Bible 200–800

Diagnostic Tests

CONTENTS

Alpha Omega Publications ®

300 North McKemy Avenue, Chandler, Arizona 85226-2618

PLACEMENT TEST for the LIFEPAC GOLD CURRICULUM

Bible 200-800

Instructions

This test is designed to aid the teacher or parent in proper placement of the student into the LIFEPAC curriculum. It has two sections: the Student Test and the Answer Key. The Answer Key is an insert in the Student Test and may be removed when testing begins. An alternate version, without the Answer Key section, is sometimes provided as part of our placement and testing services.

This is not a timed test and the student should be given an opportunity to answer each question adequately. If the student becomes bogged down and the test seems too difficult, skip to the next section. If the test is still too difficult, this child's academic skill level has been reached and testing may stop. Each test level should take no longer than one hour.

Testing should begin approximately two grade levels below the student's current or just completed grade level. For example, a student entering fifth grade [500] should begin testing at the third grade [300] level. (See Below.) Of course, a second or third grader could not test below the second grade level. This allows for proper grade level placement as well as identification of any learning gaps that the student may have.

Once the test has been administered, it is ready to be scored. The teacher or parent does all of the scoring except for those who are using a placement service. **Each section has 10 numbered questions. Each numbered question equals one point.** Use the Answer Key to mark all incorrect answers on the Student Test. Next record the total number of **correct** answers in the box beneath the LIFEPAC number in the left hand column. **When all tests have been graded, transfer the number correct by LIFEPAC to the Student Placement Worksheet on the back of the answer keys.** Then add the total number of points per grade level.

Test	Level		Test	Level
201 - 210	Level 2		601 - 610	Level 6
301 - 310	Level 3		701 - 710	Level 7
401 - 410	Level 4		801 - 810	Level 8
501 - 510	Level 5			

There are ten possible points per section. Mark the answer with an X in the square to the right of the questions.

You are God's child because He _____ you.
a. made
b. mad
c. might

You are God's child because God is your heavenly _____.
a. Mother
b. Father
c. Brother

2a. ☐
b. ☐
c. ☐

You belong to God's _____.
a. school
b. store
c. family

3a. ☐
b. ☐
c. ☐

God loves you so much that He sent his_____ to save you.
a. Brother
b. Son
c. Sister

4a. ☐
b. ☐
c. ☐

God gave you_____ to teach you how to live.
a. Jesus
b. baby
c. sister

5a. ☐
b. ☐
c. ☐

God gave you his special book, the _____ to help you.
a. reader
b. storybook
c. Bible

6a. ☐
b. ☐
c. ☐

God _____ Daniel.
a. killed
b. protected
c. hurt

7a. ☐
b. ☐
c. ☐

The king said that Daniel's God was the only_____ God.
a. happy
b. smart
c. true

8a. ☐
b. ☐
c. ☐

A new king named Darius put Daniel in the _____ den.
a. rabbits'
b. dog
c. lions'

9a. ☐
b. ☐
c. ☐

0. Daniel had faith that_____ would protect him.
a. God
b. the King
c. his friends

10a. ☐
b. ☐
c. ☐

☐

1. Moses went to live in a _____.
   a. palace
   b. basket
   c. Temple

2. Moses was _____ in a basket.
   a. playing
   b. hidden
   c. eating

3. Moses was found by _____.
   a. Miriam
   b. Mother
   c. a princess

4. When Moses was in the desert_____took care of him.
   a. God
   b. the princess
   c. Miriam

5. Moses helped some _____ at the well.
   a. sheep
   b. men
   c. girls

6. Moses went to live in _____house.
   a. a sheep
   b. Jethro's
   c. Herod's

7. God told Moses that one of his names was _____.
   a. I AM
   b. Jethro
   c. Aaron

8. One day God talked to Moses from a_____.
   a. tree
   b. burning bush
   c. burning house

9. God wanted Moses to lead His people _____Egypt.
   a. into
   b. over
   c. out of

10. Moses walked in the _____for many days.
    a. water
    b. desert
    c. snow

1a.
b.
c.

2a.
b.
c.

3a.
b.
c.

4a.
b.
c.

5a.
b.
c.

6a.
b.
c.

7a.
b.
c.

8a.
b.
c.

9a.
b.
c.

10a.
b.
c.

. Abram was a man who lived _____.
   a. yesterday
   b. long ago
   c. in America

1a. ☐
b. ☐
c. ☐

. Abram's wife was _____.
   a. Sarai
   b. Sally
   c. Susan

2a. ☐
b. ☐
c. ☐

. God told Abram and his wife to move _____.
   a. next door
   b. away
   c. nowhere

3a. ☐
b. ☐
c. ☐

. God promised Abram a _____.
   a. car
   b. horse
   c. son

4a. ☐
b. ☐
c. ☐

. Abram and Sarai waited _____ for a son.
   a. a few days
   b. many years
   c. a few weeks

5a. ☐
b. ☐
c. ☐

. God changed Abram's name to _____.
   a. Adam
   b. Abel
   c. Abraham

6a. ☐
b. ☐
c. ☐

. Abraham and Sarah had a son named _____.
   a. Isaac
   b. Abel
   c. Abram

7a. ☐
b. ☐
c. ☐

. Isaac means _____.
   a. sad
   b. mad
   c. laughter

8a. ☐
b. ☐
c. ☐

. Isaac always _____ his parents.
   a. taught
   b. obeyed
   c. hurt

9a. ☐
b. ☐
c. ☐

10. God asked Abraham to sacrifice his _____.
   a. cow
   b. lamb
   c. son

10a. ☐
b. ☐
c. ☐

1. A man who wrote part of the Old Testament was _____.
   a. Mark
   b. James
   c. Isaiah

2. The Old Testament tells us that God gave Moses _____ Commandments.
   a   ten
   b. six
   c. five

3. Isaiah was a _____.
   a. poet
   b. prophet
   c. prayer book

4. The second part of the Bible is called the _____ Testament.
   a. Old
   b. Mark
   c. New

5. The New Testament tells about _____.
   a. Jesus
   b. Isaiah
   c. Moses

6. Paul's _____ are part of the New testament.
   a. gospels
   b. letters
   c. scribes

7. Today _____ people can read the Bible in their own way of speaking.
   a. no
   b. few
   c. many

8. A person who puts the Bible into someone's way of speaking is a _____.
   a. translator
   b. telephone
   c. telegraph

9. Some people have translated the Bible into Navajo for the _____ children.
   a. English
   b. Indian
   c. poor

10. Food from heaven was called _____.
   a. bread
   b. manna
   c. son

. When David was little he took care of _____ .
  a. horses
  b. donkeys
  c. sheep

1a. ☐
b. ☐
c. ☐

. David was a _____ .
  a. fisherman
  b. shepherd
  c. school boy

2a. ☐
b. ☐
c. ☐

. David saved his sheep from a _____ with God's help.
  a. lion
  b. dog
  c. wolf

3a. ☐
b. ☐
c. ☐

. God sent _____ to David's house.
  a. Isaiah
  b. Moses
  c. Samuel

4a. ☐
b. ☐
c. ☐

. Samuel said that God wanted David to be a _____.
  a. hunter
  b. king
  c. singer

5a. ☐
b. ☐
c. ☐

. David helped King Saul by _____.
  a. killing a lion
  b. singing songs
  c. feeding sheep

6a. ☐
b. ☐
c. ☐

7. One day David saw a _____ named Goliath.
  a. horse
  b. lion
  c. giant

7a. ☐
b. ☐
c. ☐

. Goliath wanted to _____ David's people.
  a. hurt
  b. help
  c. save

8a. ☐
b. ☐
c. ☐

. God helped David to kill Goliath with a _____.
  a. sword
  b. bow and arrow
  c. stone and sling

9a. ☐
b. ☐
c. ☐

10. Psalms is near the _____ of the Bible.
  a. middle
  b. beginning
  c. end

10a. ☐
b. ☐
c. ☐

1. When God created the world, He made it out of _____.
   a. trees
   b. nothing
   c. plants

1a. ☐
b. ☐
c. ☐

2. God created the _____.
   a. sun, moon, and stars
   b. cars, houses, and toys
   c. telephones and bicycles

2a. ☐
b. ☐
c. ☐

3. God created _____.
   a. boxes
   b. pencils
   c. you

3a. ☐
b. ☐
c. ☐

4. Things that work together are called _____.
   a. alone
   b. systems
   c. single

4a. ☐
b. ☐
c. ☐

5. One of God's systems is the _____.
   a. family
   b. circus
   c. school

5a. ☐
b. ☐
c. ☐

6. In God's system, plants, animals, and people get food from the _____.
   a. table
   b. sun
   c. stars

6a. ☐
b. ☐
c. ☐

7. God told _____ to go to Nineveh.
   a. Joseph
   b. James
   c. Jonah

7a. ☐
b. ☐
c. ☐

8. Jonah was swallowed by a big _____.
   a. fish
   b. giant
   c. horse

8a. ☐
b. ☐
c. ☐

9. God _____ Jonah.
   a. left
   b. saved
   c. hurt

9a. ☐
b. ☐
c. ☐

10. Jonah was in the fish three _____.
   a. months
   b. days
   c. years

10a. ☐
b. ☐
c. ☐

1. Joseph had _____ brothers.
   a. no
   b. two
   c. many

1a. ☐
b. ☐
c. ☐

2. Joseph's father gave him a coat of _____ colors.
   a. many
   b. two
   c. three

2a. ☐
b. ☐
c. ☐

3. Joseph's brothers were _____ happy when they saw Joseph's coat.
   a. very
   b. a little
   c. not

3a. ☐
b. ☐
c. ☐

4. Joseph's brothers _____ him to a trader.
   a. sold
   b. gave
   c. hurt

4a. ☐
b. ☐
c. ☐

5. Joseph helped Pharoah and became a great _____.
   a. slave
   b. ruler
   c. dream

5a. ☐
b. ☐
c. ☐

6. Joseph helped his family when the _____ came.
   a. rain
   b. dream
   c. famine

6a. ☐
b. ☐
c. ☐

7. God helped Joseph to understand _____.
   a. cows
   b. rain
   c. dreams

7a. ☐
b. ☐
c. ☐

8. God sent Joseph to Egypt so that his family would have _____.
   a. food
   b. coats
   c. cows

8a. ☐
b. ☐
c. ☐

9. God helped Joseph become a great _____.
   a slave
   b. ruler
   c. shepherd

9a. ☐
b. ☐
c. ☐

10. God made a _____ thing out of a bad thing.
    a. good
    b. black
    c. brave

10a. ☐
b. ☐
c. ☐

1. The first family God made was Adam, Eve, _____.
   a. Abraham, and Isaac
   b. and Jacob
   c. Cain, Abel, and Seth

1a. ☐
b. ☐
c. ☐

2. Abraham's family grew when his son _____ was born.
   a. Isaac
   b. Isaiah
   c. Adam

2a. ☐
b. ☐
c. ☐

3. Isaac married _____.
   a. Eve
   b. Sarah
   c. Rebekah

3a. ☐
b. ☐
c. ☐

4. Father is the _____ of the family.
   a. brothers
   b. leader
   c. helper

4a. ☐
b. ☐
c. ☐

5. God put people in families to _____ and help each other.
   a. like
   b. hurt
   c. love

5a. ☐
b. ☐
c. ☐

6. Your mother and father are your _____.
   a. brothers
   b. parents
   c. grandparents

6a. ☐
b. ☐
c. ☐

7. God wants children to _____ their parents.
   a. obey
   b. answer
   c. feed

7a. ☐
b. ☐
c. ☐

8. God promises life will go _____ for children who obey their parents.
   a. bad
   b. well
   c. fast

8a. ☐
b. ☐
c. ☐

9. "Honour thy father and mother:" which is the first commandment with _____.
   a. love
   b. hope
   c. promise

9a. ☐
b. ☐
c. ☐

10. A new family begins when someone _____.
    a. has a birthday
    b. gets married
    c. gets a job

10a. ☐
b. ☐
c. ☐

. God's people forgot Him and became very _____.
   a. proud
   b. happy
   c. sleepy

1a. ☐
b. ☐
c. ☐

. These people tried to build a great _____ as high as heaven.
   a. house
   b. tent
   c. tower

2a. ☐
b. ☐
c. ☐

. God made the people working on the Tower of Babel _____ strangely.
   a. act
   b. talk
   c. look

3a. ☐
b. ☐
c. ☐

. Each group of people who spoke the same language became a _____.
   a. country
   b. city
   c. nation

4a. ☐
b. ☐
c. ☐

. God told Abraham that his family would become the nation of _____.
   a. Israel
   b. Isaac
   c. Isaiah

5a. ☐
b. ☐
c. ☐

. God told Abraham that _____ would be born of Abraham's family.
   a. Cain
   b. Jesus
   c. Abel

6a. ☐
b. ☐
c. ☐

. Jesus told his disciples to preach the _____ news of Jesus to all nations.
   a. bad
   b. good
   c. sad

7a. ☐
b. ☐
c. ☐

. God tells us to teach all people about _____.
   a. Jesus
   b. trees
   c. flowers

8a. ☐
b. ☐
c. ☐

. To tell other people about Jesus is a great _____.
   a. text
   b. task
   c. tank

9a. ☐
b. ☐
c. ☐

10. Jesus was born into the nation called the _____.
   a. Gentiles
   b. Philistines
   c. Jews

10a. ☐
b. ☐
c. ☐

9

1. Jesus is God's _____.
   a. father
   b. son
   c. brother

1a. ☐
b. ☐
c. ☐

2. Moses saw a burning _____.
   a. tree
   b. house
   c. bush

2a. ☐
b. ☐
c. ☐

3. Daniel was protected from the _____ by God.
   a. lions
   b. snakes
   c. dogs

3a. ☐
b. ☐
c. ☐

4. God is a _____.
   a. man
   b. spirit
   c. woman

4a. ☐
b. ☐
c. ☐

5. You can read about the Creation in the _____.
   a. New Testament
   b. Old Testament
   c. Epistles

5a. ☐
b. ☐
c. ☐

6. You can read about Jesus in the _____.
   a. New Testament
   b. Old Testament
   c. Epistles

6a. ☐
b. ☐
c. ☐

7. Paul helped start _____.
   a. wars
   b. businesses
   c. churches

7a. ☐
b. ☐
c. ☐

8. The book of Psalms was written by _____.
   a. Joseph
   b. David
   c. Moses

8a. ☐
b. ☐
c. ☐

9. God is our _____ Father.
   a. earthly
   b. friendly
   c. heavenly

9a. ☐
b. ☐
c. ☐

10 God sent _____ to die for us.
   a. Jesus
   b. Jonah
   c. Paul

10a. ☐
b. ☐
c. ☐

. Paul and Silas _____.
   a. were beaten and left dead for preaching the Gospel   1a. ☐
   b. were beaten and put in stocks in jail for casting a spirit out of a girl   b. ☐
   c. were brothers   c. ☐
   d. were shipwrecked   d. ☐

. Paul and Silas praised God _____.
   a. when they were in jail and hurting   2a. ☐
   b. only when they were happy   b. ☐
   c. only when they went to jail   c. ☐
   d. only when things were going well   d. ☐

. Because Paul and Silas praised God, _____.
   a. they were put in jail   3a. ☐
   b. they were able to heal a girl   b. ☐
   c. an earthquake happened and their jailer was saved   c. ☐
   d. they got out of their trouble and put their jailer in jail   d. ☐

. While Moses was away talking to God, the Israelites _____.
   a. prayed   4a. ☐
   b. waited patiently for him to return   b. ☐
   c. built a golden calf and worshiped it   c. ☐
   d. praised God until the mountain shook   d. ☐

. While Moses was away talking to God, the Israelites worshiped _____.
   a. the one true God   5a. ☐
   b. a man made god they could see   b. ☐
   c. nothing at all   c. ☐
   d. each other   d. ☐

. When Moses returned from talking to God, everyone who was not worshiping the true and living God _____.
   a. was sent back to Egypt   6a. ☐
   b. was made to worship Him   b. ☐
   c. was killed as punishment for his sin   c. ☐
   d. was drowned in the Red Sea   d. ☐

. Daniel was an Israelite that lived in _____.
   a. Egypt   7a. ☐
   b. Israel   b. ☐
   c. Babylon   c. ☐
   d. the United States   d. ☐

. Daniel prayed and obeyed the one true God _____.
   a. sometimes   8a. ☐
   b. whenever he needed something   b. ☐
   c. when the king told him to   c. ☐
   d. even when it was against the law   d. ☐

. The lions ate _____.
   a. Daniel   9a. ☐
   b. the king   b. ☐
   c. each other   c. ☐
   d. the wicked men   d. ☐

0. The leader of the Israelites was _____.
   a. Abraham   10a. ☐
   b. David   b. ☐
   c. Moses   c. ☐
   d. Joseph   d. ☐

1. Jesus was born in _____.
   a. Nazareth
   b. Bethlehem
   c. Jerusalem
   d. Egypt

2. Jesus was born of _____.
   a. a woman named Maria
   b. an angel named Mary
   c. a virgin named Mary
   d. an aunt to King David

3. The real father of Jesus was _____.
   a. God by the Holy Spirit
   b. Joseph
   c. David
   d. John the Baptist

4. Jesus died _____.
   a. in Jerusalem on a cross
   b. in Nazareth on a cross
   c. in Jerusalem by having His head cut off
   d. in Bethlehem from an arrow

5. Jesus died and came back to life again _____.
   a. just to prove He was God
   b. to give everlasting life to all who will receive it
   c. to make God's Word true
   d. is a fairy tale

6. Jesus went back to heaven _____.
   a. to get away from us
   b. to prepare a place for us and then He will come back to get us one day
   c. the same day he came back to life
   d. so they could not kill him again

7. The rest of this verse is _____.
   "I am the way, the truth, and life: _____."
   a. this is my beloved Son in whom I am well pleased
   b. this man is the Son of God
   c. I go to prepare a place for you
   d. no man cometh unto the father, but by me

8. Luke 2:52 is completed with these words in this order: _____."And Jesus increased (grew) in _____ and _____ and in _____ with _____ and _____."
   a. favor, wisdom, stature, man, God
   b. love, goodness, fame, God, man
   c. wisdom, stature, favor, God, man
   d. knowledge, wisdom, favor, God, people

9. The verse that is found in John 14:2 is _____.
   a. "For God so loved the world, that he gave his only begotten Son, that whosoever believeth in him, should not perish, but have everlasting life."
   b. "And she brought forth her firstborn son, and wrapped him in swaddling clothes, and laid him in a manger."
   c. "I will bless the Lord at all times: his praise shall continually be in my mouth."
   d. "In my father's house are many mansions: if it were not so, I would have told you. I go to prepare a place for you."

10. As a boy, Jesus stayed at the Temple to _____.
    a. rest awhile
    b. talk to the teachers
    c. disobey his mother
    d. see his friends

. Joseph lived in Egypt because _____.
  a. he loved the weather
  b. his family sent him there
  c. he got lost one day and ended up there
  d. slave traders took him there and sold him

. Joseph was in prison _____.
  a. because he killed a man
  b. because he got too powerful
  c. and while he was there he told two men what their dreams meant
  d. not as a prisoner, but as a guard

. Joseph's father was _____.
  a. Abraham
  b. Jacob
  c. Pharaoh
  d. Esau

. Because Joseph was governor in Egypt, he was able to _____.
  a. forget about his family
  b. find his family food when they had none
  c. telephone his family every day
  d. send presents to his family

. God helped Joseph to have favor with the Pharaoh by _____.
  a. telling the Pharaoh Joseph was a good man
  b. giving him a lot of money
  c. giving him the meaning of dreams
  d. making him a big, good-looking man

. The true sentence is _____.
  a. God wanted Joseph in Egypt so he could save his family in the famine.
  b. It was Potiphar's fault Joseph was in Egypt.
  c. The famine lasted five years
  d. Joseph was the youngest of twelve sons.

. The story of Joseph shows us _____.
  a. that God likes to make people go to prison
  b. that when people treat us badly, God does not help us
  c. that whatever happens to us God can turn it out for good
  d. that God will not help those who treat their brother badly

. " . . . All things work together for good to them that love God. . . . " is found in _____.
  a   Matthew 8:28
  b. Romans 8:28
  c. II Timothy 3:15
  d. Genesis 3:15

. When we love God, whatever happens to us, He will help _____.
  a. us if we are good
  b. us when He feels like it
  c. us when we disobey
  d. and bless us

10. God blessed everything Joseph did because Joseph _____.
  a. was a slave and a prisoner
  b. could tell what dreams meant
  c. loved and obeyed God
  d. was liked by everyone

1. Matthew, Mark, Luke, and John are called _____.
   a. Old Testament books
   b. Epistles
   c. Gospels
   d. Proverbs
2. The first and last books of the Bible are _____.
   a. Genesis and Matthew
   b. Acts and Revelation
   c. Genesis and Isaiah
   d. Genesis and Revelation
3. The list of Bible books that are in order are _____.
   a. Second Corinthians, Galatians, Ephesians, Philippians
   b. Joshua, Judges, First and Second Samuel, Esther
   c. Isaiah, Jeremiah, Ezekiel, Hosea
   d. Hebrews, James, First and Second Peter, Revelation
4. Every Christian needs to study the Bible. Three ways to study the Bible are to study _____.
   a. the whole Bible at once, a verse at a time, a word at a time
   b. one book at a time, one chapter at a time, or one verse at a time
   c. the dictionary, books about the Bible, writers of the Bible
   d. the promises and commands, the events, the Bible's cover
5. The Old Testament has _____.
   a. twenty-seven books
   b. thirteen books
   c. thirty-nine books
   d. fifty-three books
6. When you study the Bible, you need to know (1) who wrote it, (2) who it was written to, (3) where it was written, (4) what the problems were, and (5) _____.
   a. how the problems were solved
   b. what time of day it was written
   c. how many Bibles are printed each year
   d. who wrote the Bible history book
7. Second Timothy 3:16 should be completed with these words in this order: _____.
   "All scripture is given by _____ of God and is profitable for _____, for _____, for _____, for _____, in righteousness."
   a. inspiration, love, instruction,guidance, reproof
   b. command, salvation, doctrine, miracles, instruction
   c. command, direction, inspiration, instruction, promises
   d. inspiration, doctrine, reproof, correction, instruction
8. "Thy Word have I hid in mine heart, that I might not sin against thee." is found in _____.
   a. John 3:16
   b. Psalm 100:3
   c. Psalm 119:11
   d. Romans 15:4
9. In Psalm 100:3 the 3 stands for the _____.
   a. chapter
   b. verse
   c. book
   d. the page number
10. The Bible book that tells about Jesus' returning is _____.
    a. Romans
    b. Matthew
    c. Genesis
    d. Revelation

1a. ☐
b. ☐
c. ☐
d. ☐

2a. ☐
b. ☐
c. ☐
d. ☐

3a. ☐
b. ☐
c. ☐
d. ☐

4a. ☐
b. ☐
c. ☐
d. ☐

5a. ☐
b. ☐
c. ☐
d. ☐

6a. ☐
b. ☐
c. ☐
d. ☐

7a. ☐
b. ☐
c. ☐
d. ☐

8a. ☐
b. ☐
c. ☐
d. ☐

9a. ☐
b. ☐
c. ☐
d. ☐

10a. ☐
b. ☐
c. ☐
d. ☐

1. In the time of a famine, God fed Elijah by _____.
   a. raining food from heaven
   b. putting food in his cupboard
   c. sending ravens with food
   d. leading him to a special garden

   1a. ☐
   b. ☐
   c. ☐
   d. ☐

2. God helped a widow fill many pots with oil when she obeyed the word of the Lord spoken by _____.
   a. Elijah
   b. Elisha
   c. Daniel
   d. Joseph

   2a. ☐
   b. ☐
   c. ☐
   d. ☐

3. When Elijah had no water, a woman gave him water and food, too. Elijah in return _____.
   a. gave her a Bible
   b. gave her a new dress
   c. gave her oil and meal by a miracle
   d. raised her son from the dead

   3a. ☐
   b. ☐
   c. ☐
   d. ☐

4. God guided the children of Israel across the desert with _____.
   a. a cloud and with fire
   b. maps and road signs
   c. armies and scouts
   d. spies and angels

   4a. ☐
   b. ☐
   c. ☐
   d. ☐

5. God protected Shadrach, Meshach, and Abed-nego in the _____.
   a. lions den
   b. prison
   c. furnace
   d. flood

   5a. ☐
   b. ☐
   c. ☐
   d. ☐

6 God protected Shadrach, Meshach, and Abed-nego because they would not _____.
   a. worship the golden calf
   b. worship the large golden statue
   c. leave their country
   d. pray to the king

   6a. ☐
   b. ☐
   c. ☐
   d. ☐

7. Solomon obeyed God and God gave _____.
   a. riches, wisdom, and a long life
   b. problems and wars
   c. hard work and a long life
   d. whatever he wanted whenever he asked

   7a. ☐
   b. ☐
   c. ☐
   d. ☐

8. Because Samuel loved and obeyed God, God helped Samuel become a great _____.
   a. king
   b. judge
   c. prophet
   d. writer

   8a. ☐
   b. ☐
   c. ☐
   d. ☐

9. Samson disobeyed God, lost his strength, and was _____.
   a. killed
   b. put in jail
   c. beaten
   d. very sick

   9a. ☐
   b. ☐
   c. ☐
   d. ☐

10. God loves you and wants you to love and _____ Him.
   a. obey
   b. not obey
   c. give to
   d. trick

   10a. ☐
   b. ☐
   c. ☐
   d. ☐

☐

1. The Holy Spirit helped about _____ people write the Bible.
   a. 440
   b. 14
   c. 40
   d. 60

2. The Bible was written on scrolls by _____.
   a. authors
   b. scribblers
   c. children
   d. scribes

2a. ☐
   b. ☐
   c. ☐
   d. ☐

3. The Bible was written in about _____ years.
   a. 15
   b. 150
   c. 1,500
   d. 2,500

3a. ☐
   b. ☐
   c. ☐
   d. ☐

4. When King Josiah cleaned up the Temple, the men found _____.
   a. statues
   b. scrolls of the Law of Moses
   c. the New Testament
   d. food

4a. ☐
   b. ☐
   c. ☐
   d. ☐

5. When Ezra read the Law of Moses, the people _____.
   a. clapped and cheered
   b. cried
   c. danced for joy
   d. died

5a. ☐
   b. ☐
   c. ☐
   d. ☐

6. The man who helped the people rebuild the wall of Jerusalem was _____.
   a. Nehemiah
   b. Ezra
   c. Josiah
   d. Pharaoh

6a. ☐
   b. ☐
   c. ☐
   d. ☐

7. In Isaiah 7:14 God promised to send His Son. His promise came true, and it is told in _____.
   a. Acts 2:16
   b. Psalm 119:11
   c. Luke 2:7
   d. Revelation 3:20

7a. ☐
   b. ☐
   c. ☐
   d. ☐

8. A promise that God made and that has already happened is _____.
   a. "I will send the Holy Spirit to be with you"
   b. "I will come again"
   c. "The sun shall not give her light . . . "
   d. a, b, and c

8a. ☐
   b. ☐
   c. ☐
   d. ☐

9. God promises everlasting life to all who _____.
   a. believe in Him
   b. work hard
   c. go to church
   d. read the Bible

9a. ☐
   b. ☐
   c. ☐
   d. ☐

10. God sent His Son so you could have _____.
   a. a house
   b. food
   c. a LIFEPAC
   d. everlasting life

10a. ☐
   b. ☐
   c. ☐
   d. ☐

1. People who dig into ruins to study the past are called _____.
   a. professors
   b. prophets
   c. archaeologist
   d. scribes

   1a. ☐
   b. ☐
   c. ☐
   d. ☐

2. An archaeologist's tools include _____.
   a. hammer, nails, and saw
   b. paintbrush and paint
   c. paintbrush, knives and toothbrush
   d. shovel, rake, and hoe

   2a. ☐
   b. ☐
   c. ☐
   d. ☐

3. Archaeologists often dig in _____.
   a. modern cities
   b. tells
   c. mountains
   d. caves

   3a. ☐
   b. ☐
   c. ☐
   d. ☐

4. The Dead Sea Scrolls were found _____.
   a. in the Dead Sea
   b. in a cave
   c. in a grave
   d. buried in the ground

   4a. ☐
   b. ☐
   c. ☐
   d. ☐

5. The Dead Sea Scrolls tell _____.
   a. what life was like in Moses' day
   b. what life was like in the days of King David
   c. what life was like during the years between the Old and New Testaments
   d. nothing. They are too old to read

   5a. ☐
   b. ☐
   c. ☐
   d. ☐

6. Archaeology helps us understand the Bible better by _____.
   a. proving that the people and places of the Bible really were there
   b. giving us pictures
   c. writing the Bible in a way we can understand it
   d. explaining all the wars

   6a. ☐
   b. ☐
   c. ☐
   d. ☐

7. Archaeologists have proved _____.
   a. that the Bible is not true
   b. that there really was a great flood
   c. that Jesus died on a cross
   d. nothing

   7a. ☐
   b. ☐
   c. ☐
   d. ☐

8. Archaeologists have found _____.
   a. that houses were built on the walls of Jericho
   b. the Ten Commandments that God gave to Moses
   c. the old Temple
   d. the den that Daniel was in with the lions

   8a. ☐
   b. ☐
   c. ☐
   d. ☐

9. Things that are made by man and dug up by archaeologists are called _____.
   a. culture
   b. clues
   c. tells
   d. artifacts

   9a. ☐
   b. ☐
   c. ☐
   d. ☐

10. A sheet of clay or stone that people used to write on was called a _____.
    a. scroll
    b. note pad
    c. tablet
    d. plate

    10a. ☐
    b. ☐
    c. ☐
    d. ☐

1. God gave Moses _____.
   a. five commandments
   b. eight commandments
   c. ten commandments
   d. twelve commandments

1a. ☐
b. ☐
c. ☐
d. ☐

2. The commandment that says we should not desire someone else's things is _____.
   a. Thou shalt not steal
   b. Thou shalt not covet
   c. Thou shalt not kill
   d. Thou shalt not bear false witness

2a. ☐
b. ☐
c. ☐
d. ☐

3. The first three commandments tell _____.
   a. how we should treat God
   b. what to do on the Sabbath day
   c. what not to do
   d. how to treat our neighbor

3a. ☐
b. ☐
c. ☐
d. ☐

4. Abraham was a friend of God because _____.
   a. he was the father of Isaac
   b. he obeyed and believed God
   c. he was the father of a great nation
   d. he made sacrifices to God

4a. ☐
b. ☐
c. ☐
d. ☐

5. Naomi was a friend to _____.
   a. Abigail
   b. kings
   c. Ruth
   d. Esther

5a. ☐
b. ☐
c. ☐
d. ☐

6. Jonathan and David were _____.
   a. brothers
   b. kings
   c. cousins
   d. friends

6a. ☐
b. ☐
c. ☐
d. ☐

7. A person who forgives us when we have done wrong and then forgets about it is _____.
   a. a true friend
   b. our father
   c. sick
   d. paying us back

7a. ☐
b. ☐
c. ☐
d. ☐

8. The best way to make new friends is _____.
   a. to walk down the street
   b. to stand around on the playground
   c. to be friendly
   d. to play by yourself

8a. ☐
b. ☐
c. ☐
d. ☐

9. If we love God with all our heart, soul, strength, and mind, we will also _____.
   a. love our neighbor
   b. love ourself
   c. love everyone
   d. do all of these things

9a. ☐
b. ☐
c. ☐
d. ☐

10. One who shows how to act is a (n) _____.
   a. example
   b. character
   c. imitator
   d. show-off

10a. ☐
b. ☐
c. ☐
d. ☐

1. God wants us to _____.
    a. forgive others
    b. treat others just like they treat us
    c. be nice to others, but keep our toys for ourselves
    d. do all of these things

1a. ☐
b. ☐
c. ☐
d. ☐

2. Brothers and sisters are in God's family through _____.
    a. helping
    b. forgiving
    c. Jesus Christ
    d. working

2a. ☐
b. ☐
c. ☐
d. ☐

3. God says to be kind to others when _____.
    a. they are kind to you
    b. they are not kind to you
    c. you want to
    d. they go to the same church that you go to

3a. ☐
b. ☐
c. ☐
d. ☐

4. God cares for us through _____.
    a. the stars
    b. the plants
    c. people
    d. the birds

4a. ☐
b. ☐
c. ☐
d. ☐

5. We ought to love others because _____.
    a. it is a nice thing to do
    b. God loves us
    c. they will like it
    d. there is nothing else to do

5a. ☐
b. ☐
c. ☐
d. ☐

6. Even in bad times God can give us _____.
    a. peace of mind and joy
    b. friends
    c. things we need
    d. all of these things

6a. ☐
b. ☐
c. ☐
d. ☐

7. The words that are missing from this verse are _____.
"Be careful for nothing; but in _____ by prayer and supplication with _____ let your requests be made known unto _____. Philippians 4:6
    a. all things, praise, the Lord
    b. everything, thanksgiving, God
    c. everything, groanings, Jesus
    d. the night, thanksgiving, you father

7a. ☐
b. ☐
c. ☐
d. ☐

8. Ephesians 4:32 tells us _____.
    a. to make our requests known
    b. that if we believe, we will see God's glory
    c. to love on another
    d. to be kind and tenderhearted

8a. ☐
b. ☐
c. ☐
d. ☐

9. "If God so loved us, we ought also to love one another," is found in _____.
    a. John 3:16
    b. Psalm 119:11
    c. I John 4:11
    d. Romans 8:28

9a. ☐
b. ☐
c. ☐
d. ☐

10. Christians should pray about _____.
    a. everything
    b. needs only
    c. wants only
    d. nothing

10a. ☐
b. ☐
c. ☐
d. ☐

1. Abraham was the father of _____.
   a. Isaiah
   b. Isaac
   c. Joseph
   d. David

2. The Bible has _____ parts.
   a. three parts
   b. ten parts
   c. two parts
   d. six parts

3. Prophecy means to tell _____.
   a. about the future
   b. about the past
   c. about the present
   d. a lie

4. Jesus died for _____.
   a. good people only
   b. bad people only
   c. nothing
   d. our sins

5. The mother of Jesus was _____.
   a. Mary
   b. Sarah
   c. Abigail
   d. Naomi

6. The earthly father of Jesus was _____.
   a. David
   b. Joseph
   c. Paul
   d. John

7. Jesus went to the _____ when He was twelve years old.
   a. cross
   b. alter
   c. Temple
   d. store

8. The Lord's prayer is found in the Gospel of _____.
   a. Matthew
   b. Mark
   c. Luke
   d. John

9. Jesus told us to love our _____.
   a. selves
   b. family only
   c. friends only
   d. enemies

10. Isaiah was a _____.
    a. doctor
    b. prophet
    c. king
    d. shepherd

1a. ☐
b. ☐
c. ☐
d. ☐

2a. ☐
b. ☐
c. ☐
d. ☐

3a. ☐
b. ☐
c. ☐
d. ☐

4a. ☐
b. ☐
c. ☐
d. ☐

5a. ☐
b. ☐
c. ☐
d. ☐

6a. ☐
b. ☐
c. ☐
d. ☐

7a. ☐
b. ☐
c. ☐
d. ☐

8a. ☐
b. ☐
c. ☐
d. ☐

9a. ☐
b. ☐
c. ☐
d. ☐

10a. ☐
b. ☐
c. ☐
d. ☐

Peter came to know Jesus because _____.

a.   Peter heard him preach

b.   Peter saw him heal a blind man

c.   Andrew, his brother, took him to meet Jesus

d.   Peter saw a bright light and heard God speak

1a. ☐
b. ☐
c. ☐
d. ☐

After Jesus arose from the dead, three times he told Peter to _____.

a.   heal the sick

b.   feed His sheep

c.   raise the dead

d.   take care of His mother

2a. ☐
b. ☐
c. ☐
d. ☐

On the day of Pentecost _____.

a.   about fifty people repented and believed Jesus was their Saviour

b.   about five hundred people repented and believed Jesus was their Saviour

c.   many people were raised from the dead

d.   about three thousand people repented and believed Jesus was their Saviour

3a. ☐
b. ☐
c. ☐
d. ☐

After Peter preached his first sermon _____.

a.   thousands were saved, baptized, and followed the Apostles' doctrine

b.   he was stoned and run out of town

c.   he was put in prison

d.   he went out and denied Jesus

4a. ☐
b. ☐
c. ☐
d. ☐

Peter obeyed Jesus by _____.

a.   feeding His sheep (preaching)

b.   fishing

c.   going to Jerusalem

d.   helping Thomas

5a. ☐
b. ☐
c. ☐
d. ☐

We can live for God by _____.

a.   being hearers of the Word

b.   being doers of the Word

c.   fishing

d.   speaking the Word everywhere we go to everyone we meet

6a. ☐
b. ☐
c. ☐
d. ☐

Being "born again" means _____.

a.   being born all over again

b.   your brother or sister is born

c.   being born spiritually

d.   being made a Jew

7a. ☐
b. ☐
c. ☐
d. ☐

When we are born again, we _____.

a.   turn back into a baby

b.   have the Holy Spirit living within us

c.   will never sin again

d.   have to go to the hospital

8a. ☐
b. ☐
c. ☐
d. ☐

When we sin, God still loves us and will forgive us if _____.

a.   we confess the sin

b.   we quit doing it

c.   we do something kind to make up for it

d.   we forget about it

9a. ☐
b. ☐
c. ☐
d. ☐

0. We grow spiritually as _____.

a.   we eat good food

b.   the Holy Spirit works in our lives

c.   we use love, joy, peace, and long suffering

d.   we keep our face clean

10a. ☐
b. ☐
c. ☐
d. ☐

☐

1. God gave us people to love us because _____.
   a. He does not love us
   b. He did not want to be bothered with us
   c. He loves us
   d. He ran out of ideas

2. Because God loves you, He will _____.
   a. give you everything you want
   b. let you do anything you want to do
   c. give you everything you need
   d. do whatever you ask Him to do

3. We can have the knowledge of God by _____.
   a. studying God's Word
   b. praying (asking God for it)
   c. the Holy Spirit revealing it to us
   d. all of these things

4. Before Jesus went back to heaven, He promised to send a Helper. The Helper is called _____.
   a. your mom
   b. the Holy Spirit
   c. your Bible
   d. your pastor

5. God uses His knowledge to help _____.
   a. people
   b. Jesus
   c. the Holy Spirit
   d. none of these

6. God shows He cares about our actions when He _____.
   a. disciples us
   b. disappoints us
   c. disciplines us
   d. delights us

7. God sent Jesus to earth to give us _____.
   a. angels
   b. salvation
   c. suffering
   d. a, b, and c

8. Chastisement is another word for _____.
   a. presents
   b. discipline
   c. charity
   d. sin

9. The Bible says if we seek God with all our heart that we _____.
   a. please Him
   b. will get tired
   c. will find Him
   d. will not find Him because He is too big to find

10. The beginning of knowledge is _____.
    a. kindergarten
    b. a college education
    c. your parents
    d. the fear of the Lord

1. In the book of Acts, the most cruel enemy of Christians was _____.
   a. Saul
   b. Peter
   c. the rabbi
   d. the high priest

   1a. ☐
   b. ☐
   c. ☐
   d. ☐

2. A man who thought he was pleasing God by hunting down and killing Christians was _____.
   a. Stephen
   b. the rabbi
   c. Gamaliel
   d. Saul

   2a. ☐
   b. ☐
   c. ☐
   d. ☐

3. The book of Acts was written by _____.
   a. Matthew
   b. many men
   c. Luke
   d. Paul

   3a. ☐
   b. ☐
   c. ☐
   d. ☐

4. The story of how Saul became Paul is found in _____.
   a. Genesis
   b. Acts
   c. Revelation
   d. Romans

   4a. ☐
   b. ☐
   c. ☐
   d. ☐

5. Saul heard a voice say, _____.
   a. "well done, thou good and faithful servant."
   b. "Behold, the Lamb of God . . . "
   c. "This is my beloved Son. Hear ye him."
   d. "Saul, Saul, why persecutest thou me?"

   5a. ☐
   b. ☐
   c. ☐
   d. ☐

6. When Saul got up off the ground to go on to Damascus, he found that he was _____.
   a. lame
   b. blind
   c. clean
   d. dead

   6a. ☐
   b. ☐
   c. ☐
   d. ☐

7. Saul was a tentmaker from _____.
   a. Tarsus
   b. Damascus
   c. Joppa
   d. Nazareth

   7a. ☐
   b. ☐
   c. ☐
   d. ☐

8. After Jesus changed Saul to a new man named Paul, Paul went everywhere _____.
   a. persecuting Christians
   b. preaching about Jesus
   c. telling people to become Pharisees
   d. starting schools

   8a. ☐
   b. ☐
   c. ☐
   d. ☐

9. Stephen saw Jesus in heaven standing beside the Father because _____.
   a. Jesus was not dead; He had arisen and is alive now
   b. he was dreaming
   c. he was out of his head with pain
   d. he was about to die

   9a. ☐
   b. ☐
   c. ☐
   d. ☐

10. Because Jesus is alive _____.
    a. we will all live again after we die
    b. everyone that believes in Him will live forever and will not have to fear death
    c. we will never sin
    d. we will never be sick

    10a. ☐
    b. ☐
    c. ☐
    d. ☐

1. The Bible is written to _____.
   a. children only
   b. everyone
   c. adults only
   d. the High Priest

1a. ☐
 b. ☐
 c. ☐
 d. ☐

2. We should read the Bible _____.
   a. daily
   b. when we feel like it
   c. every hour
   d. when we do not have anything else to read

2a. ☐
 b. ☐
 c. ☐
 d. ☐

3. When reading the Bible, look for promises, _____.
   a. Proverbs, and Psalms
   b. problems, and possibilities
   c. commands, and principles
   d. people, and animals

3a. ☐
 b. ☐
 c. ☐
 d. ☐

4. "If we confess our sins [something God will do] . . . " is an example of a Bible _____.
   a. problem
   b. command
   c. principle
   d. promise

4a. ☐
 b. ☐
 c. ☐
 d. ☐

5. Memorizing Scripture will help you to have victory over _____.
   a. death
   b. fights
   c. sin
   d. sickness

5a. ☐
 b. ☐
 c. ☐
 d. ☐

6. The first thing to do when you memorize Scripture is _____.
   a. study it over and over
   b. copy it exactly from the Bible onto a card
   c. tell it to a friend
   d. read it once, then close the Bible and say it

6a. ☐
 b. ☐
 c. ☐
 d. ☐

7. One way to gain wisdom and to be happy is to _____.
   a. study and live by God's Proverbs
   b. work hard
   c. play hard
   d. study God's Word but do not live by it

7a. ☐
 b. ☐
 c. ☐
 d. ☐

8. It is better to have _____.
   a. gold and silver
   b. rest and peace
   c. wisdom and understanding
   d. friends and enemies

8a. ☐
 b. ☐
 c. ☐
 d. ☐

9. Proverbs teaches us not to make friends with people who _____.
   a. have hot, violent tempers
   b. have brothers
   c. have blue eyes
   d. go to church

9a. ☐
 b. ☐
 c. ☐
 d. ☐

10. Being lazy will make you _____.
   a. rich
   b. happy
   c. poor
   d. strong

10a. ☐
 b. ☐
 c. ☐
 d. ☐

1. The book of Psalms is _____.
   a. in about the middle of your Bible
   b. in the New Testament
   c. in three parts
   d. poetry

   1a. ☐
   b. ☐
   c. ☐
   d. ☐

2. The shepherd of the "Psalm of Psalms" is _____.
   a. David
   b. Moses
   c. the Lord Jesus
   d. just a shepherd

   2a. ☐
   b. ☐
   c. ☐
   d. ☐

3. The shepherd's rod and staff _____.
   a. scare the sheep
   b. comfort the sheep
   c. are left in the fold during the day
   d. are used only in an emergency

   3a. ☐
   b. ☐
   c. ☐
   d. ☐

4. When a sheep gets hurt or bruised, the shepherd anoints the bruises with _____.
   a. oil
   b. water
   c. medicine
   d. powder

   4a. ☐
   b. ☐
   c. ☐
   d. ☐

5. The Lord keeps us (his sheep) on the right path with His _____.
   a. staff
   b. goodness
   c. Word
   d. creation

   5a. ☐
   b. ☐
   c. ☐
   d. ☐

6. Mercy means _____.
   a. kindness when we do not deserve it
   b. everyone's goodness
   c. right paths
   d. laughter

   6a. ☐
   b. ☐
   c. ☐
   d. ☐

7. David protected his sheep by _____.
   a. shouting at them
   b. killing a bear and a lion
   c. singing to them
   d. writing Psalms

   7a. ☐
   b. ☐
   c. ☐
   d. ☐

8. God helped David kill _____.
   a. a soldier
   b. a giant named Saul
   c. a giant named Goliath
   d. a prophet

   8a. ☐
   b. ☐
   c. ☐
   d. ☐

9. God used Daniel to _____.
   a. teach others about God
   b. be a ruler over many people
   c. write about things that would happen in the future
   d. do all of these things

   9a. ☐
   b. ☐
   c. ☐
   d. ☐

10. Daniel honored God first at all times _____.
    a. even when it meant he would be laughed at
    b. even when it meant death
    c. because he loved God
    d. a, b, and c

    10a. ☐
    b. ☐
    c. ☐
    d. ☐

☐

1. God started the Jewish nation with _____.
   a. Noah and his family
   b. Adam and Eve
   c. Abram and Sarai
   d. Joseph and Mary

2. God led the first Jews to the land of _____.
   a. Canaan, the Promised Land
   b. Egypt, the land of sun
   c. Ur, the ancient land
   d. Galilee, the Promised Land

3. Because God came to earth as baby Jesus, Jesus is _____.
   a. the promised Jewish Saviour
   b. the promised Jewish nation
   c. no longer in heaven
   d. Abraham's promised son

4. The promised Jewish Saviour would _____.
   a. not come until everyone was looking for Him
   b. come when no one knew it
   c. save the people from their sin
   d. deliver the people from slavery

5. The greatest wonder of all God's creation is _____.
   a. the stars
   b. the human body
   c. God Himself
   d. the Grand Canyon

6. Scientists have uncovered many facts to prove, just as the Bible has said, that the earth _____.
   a. had a great Flood
   b. is flat
   c. was created in seven days
   d. is not the only planet with people

7. Everyone worships _____.
   a. wicked spirits
   b. dead relatives
   c. gods of wood and stone
   d. a god

8. Man can know the true and living God by _____.
   a. pleasing Him with good deeds
   b. receiving Jesus as their Saviour
   c. dying and going to heaven
   d. studying about Him

9. Thomas Aquinas wrote _____.
   a. poems about God
   b. psalms
   c. laws to prove God exists
   d. laws to prove there is no God

10. The correct ending to this verse is _____.
    "For the wages of sin is death; but the gift of _____." Romans 6:23
    a. God is that he hath made us and not we ourselves
    b. God is not of yourselves lest ye should boast, but of the grace of God
    c. God is eternal life through Jesus Christ our Lord
    d. God is to become the sons of God, even to them that believe on his name

1a. ☐
b. ☐
c. ☐
d. ☐

2a. ☐
b. ☐
c. ☐
d. ☐

3a. ☐
b. ☐
c. ☐
d. ☐

4a. ☐
b. ☐
c. ☐
d. ☐

5a. ☐
b. ☐
c. ☐
d. ☐

6a. ☐
b. ☐
c. ☐
d. ☐

7a. ☐
b. ☐
c. ☐
d. ☐

8a. ☐
b. ☐
c. ☐
d. ☐

9a. ☐
b. ☐
c. ☐
d. ☐

10a. ☐
b. ☐
c. ☐
d. ☐

1. The great rivers of the Fertile Crescent are _____. **407**
   a. Tigris, Euphrates, and Nile   1a. ☐
   b. Tigris and Euphrates   b. ☐
   c. Tigris, Euphrates, and Jordan   c. ☐
   d. Jordan, Tigris, and Nile   d. ☐

2. The land of the Fertile Crescent had much farming because of _____.
   a. snowfall   2a. ☐
   b. rich soil from the many rivers   b. ☐
   c. people living there   c. ☐
   d. a long growing season   d. ☐

3. The terrain of Canaan is _____.
   a. desert   3a. ☐
   b. rocky hills   b. ☐
   c. coastal plains   c. ☐
   d. a, b, and c   d. ☐

4. Nomads are people who _____.
   a. live in cities   4a. ☐
   b. travel from place to place fighting   b. ☐
   c. travel from place to place with their herds   c. ☐
   d. have no names   d. ☐

5. Farmers of Canaan depended on _____ for good crops.
   a. the former and latter rains   5a. ☐
   b. good camels   b. ☐
   c. slave labor   c. ☐
   d. each other   d. ☐

6. In the rocky high country people raised _____.
   a. camels   6a. ☐
   b. sheep and goats   b. ☐
   c. horses and cattle   c. ☐
   d. crops   d. ☐

7. Bible lands were called _____.
   a. the war path   7a. ☐
   b. the Jewish empire   b. ☐
   c. the world's playground   c. ☐
   d. the crossroads of the world   d. ☐

8. When the Jewish nation left Egypt and crossed the Red Sea, they wandered around many months in _____.
   a. the valley of Horeb   8a. ☐
   b. Canaan   b. ☐
   c. the Sinai Peninsula   c. ☐
   d. the land of the Philistines   d. ☐

9. Abraham was from a city named _____.
   a. Ur of Mesopotamia   9a. ☐
   b. Goshen of Egypt   b. ☐
   c. Dan of the Negeb   c. ☐
   d. he had no city   d. ☐

10. The _____ River flows southward below sea level to the _____.
   a. Nile, Red Sea   10a. ☐
   b. Jordan, Nile River   b. ☐
   c. Tigris, Euphrates River   c. ☐
   d. Jordan, Dead Sea   d. ☐

☐

1. You are important to God because _____.
   a. your are made in His image
   b. God loves you
   c. Jesus gave His life for you
   d. of all these reasons

2. Because God knows when a little sparrow falls from a tree, He _____.
   a. is too busy to care about you
   b. is interested in only the animals
   c. also knows all about you
   d. reaches out and takes care of it

   2a. ☐
   b. ☐
   c. ☐
   d. ☐

3. The part of you that is made in God's image is _____.
   a. your body
   b. your personality
   c. the parts that cannot be seen with the eye
   d. a, b, and c

   3a. ☐
   b. ☐
   c. ☐
   d. ☐

4. God loves, thinks, and decides what to do. You are made in His image and you, too, do those things with your _____.
   a. heart, mind, and will
   b. emotions, brain, and body
   c. head, arms, and legs
   d. friends

   4a. ☐
   b. ☐
   c. ☐
   d. ☐

5. God gives us _____.
   a. what we need
   b. only good gifts
   c. both a and b
   d. gifts when we are good

   5a. ☐
   b. ☐
   c. ☐
   d. ☐

6. When you are afraid, you should _____.
   a. hide
   b. try to be brave
   c. ask God for peace
   d. call for God because He does not know where you are

   6a. ☐
   b. ☐
   c. ☐
   d. ☐

7. When you trust Jesus as your Saviour, God takes you for His own. He _____.
   a. adopts you
   b. baptizes you
   c. takes you to heaven
   d. gives you presents

   7a. ☐
   b. ☐
   c. ☐
   d. ☐

8. We become a part of God's family when _____.
   a. we are born
   b. we are adopted by God
   c. we die
   d. Mother says we are

   8a. ☐
   b. ☐
   c. ☐
   d. ☐

9. God has _____.
   a. no beginning and no end
   b. a beginning
   c. a beginning and will have an end
   d. lots of grandchildren

   9a. ☐
   b. ☐
   c. ☐
   d. ☐

10. Your worth comes from _____.
    a. your parents
    b. your teachers
    c. God
    d. what others think of you

    10a. ☐
    b. ☐
    c. ☐
    d. ☐

1. Mark 16:15 says _____.
    a. "For God so loved the world, that he gave his only begotten Son . . . "
    b. "Go ye into all the world, and preach the gospel to every creature."
    c. "Thy word have I hid in my heart, that I might not sin against Thee."
    d. "Because I live, ye shall live also."

1a. ☐
b. ☐
c. ☐
d. ☐

2. God has given only one way to _____.
    a. witness
    b. please God
    c. get into God's family
    d. die

2a. ☐
b. ☐
c. ☐
d. ☐

3. We can witness with our _____.
    a. words
    b. actions
    c. lives
    d. a, b, and c

3a. ☐
b. ☐
c. ☐
d. ☐

4. When Jesus talked to the Samaritan woman at the well, she wanted _____.
    a. to hear all the things she had ever done
    b. the disciples to talk to her too
    c. Jesus to like her
    d. Jesus to give her "living water"

4a. ☐
b. ☐
c. ☐
d. ☐

5. *Death* means _____.
    a. with God
    b. separated from God
    c. sin
    d. punishment

5a. ☐
b. ☐
c. ☐
d. ☐

6. Sin (disobeying God) causes _____.
    a. happiness
    b. life
    c. death
    d. a, b, and c

6a. ☐
b. ☐
c. ☐
d. ☐

7. We show God we love him when we _____.
    a. obey Him
    b. love others
    c. do what we want
    d. both a and b

7a. ☐
b. ☐
c. ☐
d. ☐

8. When we keep God's commandments, we _____.
    a. are loving Him
    b. are doing what is best for us
    c. are making life better for all
    d. do all of these things

8a. ☐
b. ☐
c. ☐
d. ☐

9. "Thy word have I hid in my heart, that I might not sin against Thee," is found in _____.
    a. John 13:35
    b. Psalm 119:11
    c. John 14:15
    d. I Thessalonians 5:18

9a. ☐
b. ☐
c. ☐
d. ☐

10. "By this shall all men know that ye are my disciples, if ye have love one to another," is found in

_____.
    a. John 3:16
    b. John 14:19
    c. John 13:35
    d. I John 4:7

10a. ☐
b. ☐
c. ☐
d. ☐

☐

1. We can be "born again" because _____.
   a. Nicodemus asked Jesus about it
   b. Moses held up a bronze serpent for the people to look at
   c. Jesus died for us and arose to give us His life
   d. we are so good that God just gives us a new life

1a. ☐
b. ☐
c. ☐
d. ☐

2. A baby grows by drinking milk. A new Christian grows by _____.
   a. hearing and doing the Word
   b. drinking milk
   c. being good
   d. sleeping

2a. ☐
b. ☐
c. ☐
d. ☐

3. God's knowledge _____.
   a. is known only in heaven
   b. is known only by God
   c. is never revealed to people
   d. covers everything

3a. ☐
b. ☐
c. ☐
d. ☐

4. The Holy Spirit _____.
   a. prays for you
   b. helps you understand God's Word
   c. gives you heavenly thoughts and desires
   d. does all of these things

4a. ☐
b. ☐
c. ☐
d. ☐

5. Saul thought that the teaching of the Resurrection was _____.
   a. a fairy tale
   b. powerful
   c. a lie
   d. funny

5a. ☐
b. ☐
c. ☐
d. ☐

6. When Saul was traveling to Damascus, he was knocked to the ground by _____.
   a. a bright light
   b. an angel
   c. robbers
   d. a tree branch

6a. ☐
b. ☐
c. ☐
d. ☐

7. Paul wrote many letters to the churches he had started through the ideas and help of _____.
   a. Gamaliel
   b. Peter
   c. the Holy Spirit
   d. the High Priest

7a. ☐
b. ☐
c. ☐
d. ☐

8. It is best to read the Bible _____.
   a. at a desk
   b. outdoors
   c. in the car
   d. late at night

8a. ☐
b. ☐
c. ☐
d. ☐

9. Memorizing Scripture will help you to not be _____.
   a. happy
   b. tall
   c. silly
   d. afraid

9a. ☐
b. ☐
c. ☐
d. ☐

10. You can glorify God by _____.
    a. thinking you are the best
    b. loving and obeying Him
    c. reading His Word and doing whatever you want to do
    d. being proud

10a. ☐
b. ☐
c. ☐
d. ☐

1. The man who called himself the "disciple whom Jesus loved" was _____.
   a. John \square 1a. ☐
   b. Paul b. ☐
   c. David c. ☐
   d. Abraham d. ☐
2. The woman who prayed and believed God for a son was _____.
   a. Ruth 2a. ☐
   b. Hannah b. ☐
   c. Eve c. ☐
   d. Esther d. ☐
3. God commanded Abraham to sacrifice his son Isaac. Abraham was righteous in God's sight because he _____.
   a. disobeyed 3a. ☐
   b. discussed this with friends b. ☐
   c. obeyed c. ☐
   d. sacrificed a lamb d. ☐
4. Ruth was righteous in God's sight because _____.
   a. She was Naomi's daughter-in-law 4a. ☐
   b. her husband died and left her alone b. ☐
   c. she was a hard worker c. ☐
   d. she realized Naomi's God was the one true God and she chose to live for Him d. ☐
5. Jonah was commanded by God to go to Nineveh and tell the people about God. Jonah disobeyed God at first because _____.
   a. he got on the wrong ship 5a. ☐
   b. he did not really love the people of Nineveh and did not care what happened to them b. ☐
   c. he got very sick c. ☐
   d. he wanted to make sure God really wanted him to go d. ☐
6. God loved and used David. David was a "man after God's own heart." David, however, _____.
   a. committed some great sins 6a. ☐
   b. never sinned b. ☐
   c. killed Saul c. ☐
   d. was not a good king d. ☐
7. John is known as the Apostle of _____.
   a. wisdom 7a. ☐
   b. love b. ☐
   c. obedience c. ☐
   d. faith d. ☐
8. Because of Hannah's prayers and faith, God gave her a son. Hannah dedicated Samuel to God. Samuel became a priest, and God _____.
   a. blessed Hannah with many riches 8a. ☐
   b. did not allow Hannah to die b. ☐
   c. gave Hannah other children c. ☐
   d. gave Hannah the Promised Land d. ☐
9. If a child of God sins, he should _____.
   a. give up hope 9a. ☐
   b. give more money in the offering b. ☐
   c. pray for forgiveness c. ☐
   d. keep on sinning d. ☐
10. Living the Christian life is like running a race. Living the Christian life as God planned _____.
   a. is easy 10a. ☐
   b. attracts a lot of people to cheer a Christian on b. ☐
   c. makes some Christians winners and some losers c. ☐
   d. takes commitment and endurance d. ☐

1. Angels are _____ beings.
   a. physical   1a. ☐
   b. spiritual   b. ☐
   c. natural   c. ☐
   d. unreal   d. ☐
2. Angels are invisible because they have no _____.
   a. spirits   2a. ☐
   b. bodies   b. ☐
   c. voices   c. ☐
   d. emotions   d. ☐
3. Some angels are evil and follow _____.
   a. men   3a. ☐
   b. Satan   b. ☐
   c. Gabriel   c. ☐
   d. the world   d. ☐
4. The multitude of God's angels are called the angel _____.
   a. hosts   4a. ☐
   b. flock   b. ☐
   c. fleet   c. ☐
   d. army   d. ☐
5. An angel told Abraham _____.
   a. not to give Lot his choice of land   5a. ☐
   b. to go to Egypt   b. ☐
   c. not to offer Isaac as a sacrifice   c. ☐
   d. to lie to Pharaoh about his wife   d. ☐
6. While Elijah was tired and discouraged, an angel came and _____.
   a. protected him   6a. ☐
   b. guided him to water   b. ☐
   c. provided meals for him   c. ☐
   d. released him from prison   d. ☐
7. Mary was visited by the angel Gabriel and was told she would have a son, and His name would be _____.
   a. Jesus   7a. ☐
   b. John   b. ☐
   c. Michael   c. ☐
   d. Samuel   d. ☐
8. After Jesus was tempted by the devil, angels came and _____.
   a. defeated Satan   8a. ☐
   b. sang to Jesus   b. ☐
   c. strengthened Jesus   c. ☐
   d. gave directions to Jesus   d. ☐
9. Sometimes God uses angels to supply our _____.
   a. desires   9a. ☐
   b. luxuries   b. ☐
   c. needs   c. ☐
   d. forgiveness   d. ☐
10. Angels are sent to help the _____ of salvation.
   a. heirs   10a. ☐
   b. laws   b. ☐
   c. forgiveness   c. ☐
   d. plan   d. ☐

1. *Omnipresent* means _____.
   a. sometimes present
   b. never present
   c. present everywhere at the same time
   d. often present

2. Complete this Bible verse. (Psalm 145:18) "The Lord is _____ unto all them that call upon him . . . ."
   a. not listening
   b. far away
   c. nigh (near)
   d. willing

3. "He telleth the number of the stars." (Psalm 147:4) This verse means that God's _____ is everywhere.
   a. knowledge
   b. faithfulness
   c. love
   d. hope

4. When you need to decide if something is right or wrong, good or bad, God's _____ is there to guide you.
   a. truth
   b. faithfulness
   c. love
   d. hope

5. The man in Bible days who put a fleece out to test God's presence was _____.
   a. Adam
   b. Gideon
   c. Moses
   d. Joshua

6. God's presence with the three Hebrew men in the furnace was _____.
   a. not obvious to those watching
   b. not real
   c. a testimony to everyone watching
   d. not enough to save them

7. The man who felt God's presence guide him through dense jungles and protect him from fierce animals and unfriendly natives in Africa was _____.
   a. David Livingstone
   b. David Brainerd
   c. Gideon
   d. John Cabot

8. Gladys Aylward was a missionary to China. She felt God's presence when she had _____.
   a. to travel with one hundred children over the mountains
   b. to sail a large ship alone
   c. to fight for China's independence
   d. to learn a new language

9. God is present to hear, to see, and _____.
   a. to follow
   b. to speak
   c. to leave
   d. to yell

10. God speaks through _____.
    a. the Holy Spirit
    b. sin
    c. the story of Israel
    d. creation

1. The theme of the whole Bible is _____.
   a. salvation
   b. sin
   c. the story of Israel
   d. creation

2. The main character of the Bible is _____.
   a. Israel
   b. man
   c. Jesus Christ
   d. Paul

   2a. ☐
   b. ☐
   c. ☐
   d. ☐

3. The Old Testament is divided into three sections: History, Poetry, and _____.
   a. Prophecy
   b. Genealogy
   c. Psalms
   d. Letters

   3a. ☐
   b. ☐
   c. ☐
   d. ☐

4. The Old Testament contains the history of _____.
   a. Eden
   b. Israel
   c. the United States
   d. Egypt

   4a. ☐
   b. ☐
   c. ☐
   d. ☐

5. The four Gospels tell the story of _____.
   a. Jesus' birth, life, death, and resurrection
   b. Jesus' birth
   c. Jesus' death
   d. Jesus' resurrection

   5a. ☐
   b. ☐
   c. ☐
   d. ☐

6. The four sections of the New Testament are Prophecy, Gospels, History, and _____.
   a. Poetry
   b. Epistles
   c. Law
   d. Genealogy

   6a. ☐
   b. ☐
   c. ☐
   d. ☐

7. The list of Bible books that is in correct order is _____.
   a. Hebrews, Colossians, First Peter, Second Peter
   b. Job, Exodus, Jeremiah, Ruth
   c. Ezra, Joshua, Proverbs, Psalms
   d. Galatians, Ephesians, Philippians, Colossians

   7a. ☐
   b. ☐
   c. ☐
   d. ☐

8. The first book of the Bible is _____.
   a. Exodus
   b. Genesis
   c. Matthew
   d. Job

   8a. ☐
   b. ☐
   c. ☐
   d. ☐

9. In Psalm 119:105 God's Word is described as _____.
   a. a book
   b. a lamp and a light
   c. two edged sword
   d. tablets of stone

   9a. ☐
   b. ☐
   c. ☐
   d. ☐

10. Second Peter 1:20 and 21 tells us that God's Word was written _____.
    a. by men moved by the Holy Spirit
    b. by men
    c. by Moses
    d. in a short amount of time

    10a. ☐
    b. ☐
    c. ☐
    d. ☐

	201	202	203	204	205
1	a	a	b	c	c
2	b	b	a	a	b
3	c	c	b	b	a
4	b	a	c	c	c
5	a	c	b	a	b
6	c	b	c	b	b
7	b	a	a	c	c
8	c	b	c	a	a
9	c	c	b	b	c
10	a	b	c	b	a

	206	207	208	209	210
1a.	□	□	□	■	□
b.	■	□	□	□	■
c.	□	■	■	□	□
2a.	■	■	■	□	□
b.	□	□	□	□	□
c.	□	□	□	■	■
3a.	□	□	□	□	■
b.	□	□	□	■	□
c.	■	■	■	□	□
4a.	□	■	□	□	□
b.	■	□	■	□	■
c.	□	□	□	■	□
5a.	■	□	□	■	□
b.	□	■	□	□	■
c.	□	□	■	□	□
6a.	□	□	□	□	■
b.	■	□	■	■	□
c.	□	■	□	□	□
7a.	□	□	■	□	□
b.	□	□	□	■	□
c.	■	■	□	□	■
8a.	■	■	□	■	□
b.	□	□	■	□	■
c.	□	□	□	□	□
9a.	□	□	□	□	□
b.	■	■	□	■	□
c.	□	□	■	□	■
10a.	□	■	□	□	■
b.	■	□	■	□	□
c.	□	□	□	■	□

AK-2

	301	302	303	304	305
1	b	b	d	c	c
2	a	c	c	d	b
3	c	a	b	a	d
4	c	a	b	b	a
5	b	b	c	c	c
6	c	b	a	a	b
7	c	d	c	d	a
8	d	c	b	c	c
9	d	d	d	b	b
10	c	b	c	d	a

	306	307	308	309	310
1a	□	□	□	■	□
b	□	□	□	□	■
c	■	■	■	□	□
d	□	□	□	□	□
2a	□	□	□	□	□
b	□	□	■	□	□
c	□	■	□	■	■
d	■	□	□	□	□
3a	□	□	■	□	■
b	□	■	□	■	□
c	■	□	□	□	□
d	□	□	□	□	□
4a	□	□	□	□	□
b	■	■	■	□	□
c	□	□	□	■	□
d	□	□	□	□	■
5a	□	□	□	□	■
b	■	□	□	■	□
c	□	■	■	□	□
d	□	□	□	□	□
6a	■	■	□	□	□
b	□	□	□	□	■
c	□	□	□	□	□
d	□	□	■	■	□
7a	□	□	■	□	□
b	□	■	□	■	□
c	■	□	□	□	■
d	□	□	□	□	□
8a	■	■	□	□	■
b	□	□	□	□	□
c	□	□	■	□	□
d	□	□	□	■	□
9a	■	□	□	□	□
b	□	□	□	□	□
c	□	□	□	■	□
d	□	■	■	□	■
10a	□	□	■	■	□
b	□	□	□	□	■
c	□	■	□	□	□
d	■	□	□	□	□

401

1a. ☐
 b. ☐
 c. ■
 d. ☐

2a. ☐
 b. ■
 c. ☐
 d. ☐

3a. ☐
 b. ☐
 c. ☐
 d. ■

4a. ■
 b. ☐
 c. ☐
 d. ☐

5a. ■
 b. ☐
 c. ☐
 d. ☐

6a. ☐
 b. ■
 c. ☐
 d. ☐

7a. ☐
 b. ☐
 c. ■
 d. ☐

8a. ☐
 b. ■
 c. ☐
 d. ☐

9a. ■
 b. ☐
 c. ☐
 d. ☐

10a. ☐
 b. ■
 c. ☐
 d. ☐

402

1a. ☐
 b. ☐
 c. ■
 d. ☐

2a. ☐
 b. ☐
 c. ■
 d. ☐

3a. ☐
 b. ☐
 c. ☐
 d. ■

4a. ☐
 b. ■
 c. ☐
 d. ☐

5a. ■
 b. ☐
 c. ☐
 d. ☐

6a. ☐
 b. ☐
 c. ■
 d. ☐

7a. ☐
 b. ■
 c. ☐
 d. ☐

8a. ☐
 b. ■
 c. ☐
 d. ☐

9a. ☐
 b. ☐
 c. ■
 d. ☐

10a. ☐
 b. ☐
 c. ☐
 d. ■

403

1a. ■
 b. ☐
 c. ☐
 d. ☐

2a. ☐
 b. ☐
 c. ☐
 d. ■

3a. ☐
 b. ☐
 c. ■
 d. ☐

4a. ☐
 b. ■
 c. ☐
 d. ☐

5a. ☐
 b. ☐
 c. ☐
 d. ■

6a. ☐
 b. ■
 c. ☐
 d. ☐

7a. ■
 b. ☐
 c. ☐
 d. ☐

8a. ☐
 b. ■
 c. ☐
 d. ☐

9a. ■
 b. ☐
 c. ☐
 d. ☐

10a. ☐
 b. ■
 c. ☐
 d. ☐

404

1a. ☐
 b. ■
 c. ☐
 d. ☐

2a. ■
 b. ☐
 c. ☐
 d. ☐

3a. ☐
 b. ☐
 c. ■
 d. ☐

4a. ☐
 b. ☐
 c. ☐
 d. ■

5a. ☐
 b. ☐
 c. ■
 d. ☐

6a. ☐
 b. ■
 c. ☐
 d. ☐

7a. ■
 b. ☐
 c. ☐
 d. ☐

8a. ☐
 b. ☐
 c. ■
 d. ☐

9a. ■
 b. ☐
 c. ☐
 d. ☐

10a. ☐
 b. ☐
 c. ■
 d. ☐

405

1a. ■
 b. ☐
 c. ☐
 d. ☐

2a. ☐
 b. ☐
 c. ■
 d. ☐

3a. ☐
 b. ■
 c. ☐
 d. ☐

4a. ■
 b. ☐
 c. ☐
 d. ☐

5a. ☐
 b. ☐
 c. ■
 d. ☐

6a. ■
 b. ☐
 c. ☐
 d. ☐

7a. ☐
 b. ■
 c. ☐
 d. ☐

8a. ☐
 b. ☐
 c. ■
 d. ☐

9a. ☐
 b. ☐
 c. ☐
 d. ■

10a. ☐
 b. ☐
 c. ☐
 d. ■

	406	407	408	409	410
1	c	c	d	b	c
2	a	b	c	c	a
3	a	d	c	d	d
4	c	c	a	d	d
5	b	a	c	b	c
6	a	b	c	c	a
7	d	d	a	d	c
8	b	c	b	d	a
9	c	a	a	b	d
10	c	d	c	c	b

AK-6

501	502	503	504	505
1a. ■	1a. ☐	1a. ☐	1a. ■	1a. ☐
b. ☐	b. ■	b. ☐	b. ☐	b. ☐
c. ☐	c. ☐	c. ■	c. ☐	c. ■
d. ☐	d. ☐	d. ☐	d. ☐	d. ☐
2a. ☐	2a. ☐	2a. ☐	2a. ☐	2a. ☐
b. ■	b. ■	b. ☐	b. ☐	b. ☐
c. ☐	c. ☐	c. ■	c. ■	c. ☐
d. ☐	d. ☐	d. ☐	d. ☐	d. ■
3a. ☐	3a. ☐	3a. ■	3a. ■	3a. ☐
b. ☐	b. ■	b. ☐	b. ☐	b. ■
c. ■	c. ☐	c. ☐	c. ☐	c. ☐
d. ☐	d. ☐	d. ☐	d. ☐	d. ☐
4a. ☐	4a. ■	4a. ■	4a. ☐	4a. ☐
b. ☐	b. ☐	b. ☐	b. ■	b. ☐
c. ☐	c. ☐	c. ☐	c. ☐	c. ☐
d. ■	d. ☐	d. ☐	d. ☐	d. ■
5a. ☐	5a. ☐	5a. ☐	5a. ■	5a. ☐
b. ■	b. ☐	b. ■	b. ☐	b. ■
c. ☐	c. ■	c. ☐	c. ☐	c. ☐
d. ☐	d. ☐	d. ☐	d. ☐	d. ☐
6a. ■	6a. ☐	6a. ☐	6a. ☐	6a. ■
b. ☐	b. ☐	b. ☐	b. ■	b. ☐
c. ☐	c. ■	c. ■	c. ☐	c. ☐
d. ☐	d. ☐	d. ☐	d. ☐	d. ☐
7a. ☐	7a. ■	7a. ■	7a. ☐	7a. ☐
b. ■	b. ☐	b. ☐	b. ☐	b. ☐
c. ☐	c. ☐	c. ☐	c. ☐	c. ☐
d. ☐	d. ☐	d. ☐	d. ■	d. ■
8a. ☐	8a. ☐	8a. ■	8a. ☐	8a. ■
b. ☐	b. ☐	b. ☐	b. ■	b. ☐
c. ■	c. ■	c. ☐	c. ☐	c. ☐
d. ☐	d. ☐	d. ☐	d. ☐	d. ☐
9a. ☐	9a. ☐	9a. ☐	9a. ☐	9a. ■
b. ☐	b. ☐	b. ■	b. ■	b. ☐
c. ■	c. ■	c. ☐	c. ☐	c. ☐
d. ☐	d. ☐	d. ☐	d. ☐	d. ☐
10a. ☐	10a. ■	10a. ■	10a. ■	10a. ☐
b. ☐	b. ☐	b. ☐	b. ☐	b. ■
c. ☐	c. ☐	c. ☐	c. ☐	c. ☐
d. ■	d. ☐	d. ☐	d. ☐	d. ☐

506	507	508	509	510
1a. ☐	1a. ☐	1a. ☐	1a. ☐	1a. ■
b. ■	b. ■	b. ☐	b. ☐	b. ☐
c. ☐	c. ☐	c. ■	c. ■	c. ☐
d. ☐	d. ☐	d. ☐	d. ☐	d. ☐
2a. ■	2a. ☐	2a. ☐	2a. ■	2a. ■
b. ☐	b. ☐	b. ☐	b. ☐	b. ☐
c. ☐	c. ■	c. ■	c. ☐	c. ☐
d. ☐	d. ☐	d. ☐	d. ☐	d. ☐
3a. ☐	3a. ■	3a. ■	3a. ☐	3a. ☐
b. ☐	b. ☐	b. ☐	b. ☐	b. ■
c. ☐	c. ☐	c. ☐	c. ■	c. ☐
d. ■	d. ☐	d. ☐	d. ☐	d. ☐
4a. ■	4a. ☐	4a. ☐	4a. ■	4a. ■
b. ☐	b. ☐	b. ☐	b. ☐	b. ☐
c. ☐	c. ☐	c. ■	c. ☐	c. ☐
d. ☐	d. ■	d. ☐	d. ☐	d. ☐
5a. ☐	5a. ☐	5a. ■	5a. ☐	5a. ☐
b. ☐	b. ■	b. ☐	b. ☐	b. ☐
c. ■	c. ☐	c. ☐	c. ■	c. ☐
d. ☐	d. ☐	d. ☐	d. ☐	d. ■
6a. ■	6a. ■	6a. ☐	6a. ☐	6a. ■
b. ☐	b. ☐	b. ☐	b. ■	b. ☐
c. ☐	c. ☐	c. ■	c. ☐	c. ☐
d. ☐	d. ☐	d. ☐	d. ☐	d. ☐
7a. ■	7a. ☐	7a. ■	7a. ☐	7a. ☐
b. ☐	b. ■	b. ☐	b. ☐	b. ☐
c. ☐	c. ☐	c. ☐	c. ☐	c. ☐
d. ☐	d. ☐	d. ☐	d. ■	d. ■
8a. ☐	8a. ☐	8a. ☐	8a. ■	8a. ☐
b. ☐	b. ■	b. ■	b. ☐	b. ■
c. ■	c. ☐	c. ☐	c. ☐	c. ☐
d. ☐	d. ☐	d. ☐	d. ☐	d. ☐
9a. ■	9a. ■	9a. ☐	9a. ■	9a. ☐
b. ☐	b. ☐	b. ■	b. ☐	b. ☐
c. ☐	c. ☐	c. ☐	c. ☐	c. ■
d. ☐	d. ☐	d. ☐	d. ☐	d. ☐
10a. ■	10a. ☐	10a. ■	10a. ☐	10a. ☐
b. ☐	b. ■	b. ☐	b. ■	b. ☐
c. ☐	c. ☐	c. ☐	c. ☐	c. ☐
d. ☐	d. ☐	d. ☐	d. ☐	d. ■

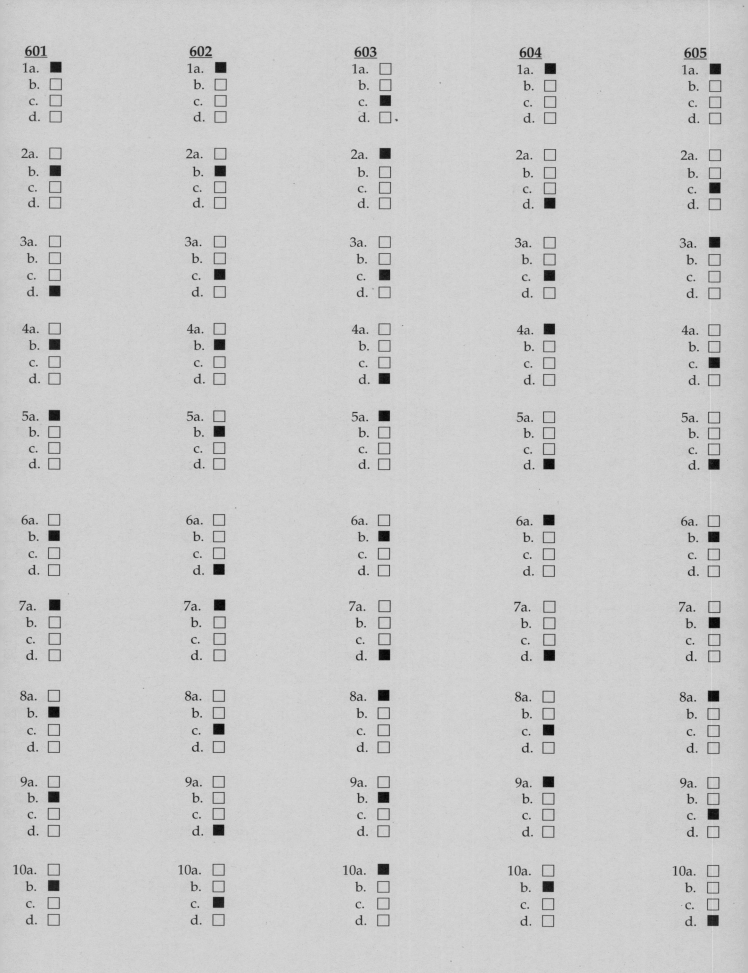

601

1a. ■ b. ☐ c. ☐ d. ☐
2a. ☐ b. ■ c. ☐ d. ☐
3a. ☐ b. ☐ c. ☐ d. ■
4a. ☐ b. ■ c. ☐ d. ☐
5a. ■ b. ☐ c. ☐ d. ☐
6a. ☐ b. ■ c. ☐ d. ☐
7a. ■ b. ☐ c. ☐ d. ☐
8a. ☐ b. ■ c. ☐ d. ☐
9a. ☐ b. ■ c. ☐ d. ☐
10a. ☐ b. ■ c. ☐ d. ☐

602

1a. ■ b. ☐ c. ☐ d. ☐
2a. ☐ b. ■ c. ☐ d. ☐
3a. ☐ b. ☐ c. ■ d. ☐
4a. ☐ b. ■ c. ☐ d. ☐
5a. ☐ b. ■ c. ☐ d. ☐
6a. ☐ b. ☐ c. ☐ d. ■
7a. ■ b. ☐ c. ☐ d. ☐
8a. ☐ b. ☐ c. ■ d. ☐
9a. ☐ b. ☐ c. ☐ d. ■
10a. ☐ b. ☐ c. ■ d. ☐

603

1a. ☐ b. ☐ c. ■ d. ☐
2a. ■ b. ☐ c. ☐ d. ☐
3a. ☐ b. ☐ c. ■ d. ☐
4a. ☐ b. ☐ c. ☐ d. ■
5a. ■ b. ☐ c. ☐ d. ☐
6a. ☐ b. ■ c. ☐ d. ☐
7a. ☐ b. ☐ c. ☐ d. ■
8a. ■ b. ☐ c. ☐ d. ☐
9a. ☐ b. ■ c. ☐ d. ☐
10a. ■ b. ☐ c. ☐ d. ☐

604

1a. ■ b. ☐ c. ☐ d. ☐
2a. ☐ b. ☐ c. ☐ d. ■
3a. ☐ b. ☐ c. ■ d. ☐
4a. ■ b. ☐ c. ☐ d. ☐
5a. ☐ b. ☐ c. ☐ d. ■
6a. ■ b. ☐ c. ☐ d. ☐
7a. ☐ b. ☐ c. ☐ d. ■
8a. ☐ b. ☐ c. ■ d. ☐
9a. ■ b. ☐ c. ☐ d. ☐
10a. ☐ b. ■ c. ☐ d. ☐

605

1a. ■ b. ☐ c. ☐ d. ☐
2a. ☐ b. ☐ c. ■ d. ☐
3a. ■ b. ☐ c. ☐ d. ☐
4a. ☐ b. ☐ c. ■ d. ☐
5a. ☐ b. ☐ c. ☐ d. ■
6a. ☐ b. ■ c. ☐ d. ☐
7a. ☐ b. ■ c. ☐ d. ☐
8a. ■ b. ☐ c. ☐ d. ☐
9a. ☐ b. ☐ c. ■ d. ☐
10a. ☐ b. ☐ c. ☐ d. ■

	606	607	608	609	610
1	a	d	a	d	c
2	b	c	c	a	c
3	a	b	a	b	c
4	c	a	a	b	a
5	c	a	d	d	b
6	a	d	c	b	c
7	a	b	d	a	b
8	b	c	c	a	c
9	a	b	c	d	b
10	d	d	a	b	b

	701	702	703	704	705
1	c	c	b	d	d
2	d	b	a	b	b
3	d	c	c	d	a
4	b	a	d	d	c
5	a	b	c	b	d
6	c	a	c	c	b
7	c	d	b	d	d
8	d	c	a	c	b
9	c	b	c	a	a
10	a	c	b	b	a

706	707	708	709	710
1a. ☐ b. ■ c. ☐ d. ☐	1a. ☐ b. ☐ c. ■ d. ☐	1a. ☐ b. ☐ c. ☐ d. ■	1a. ■ b. ☐ c. ☐ d. ☐	1a. ☐ b. ☐ c. ■ d. ☐
2a. ☐ b. ☐ c. ☐ d. ■	2a. ■ b. ☐ c. ☐ d. ☐	2a. ☐ b. ☐ c. ■ d. ☐	2a. ☐ b. ☐ c. ■ d. ☐	2a. ■ b. ☐ c. ☐ d. ☐
3a. ☐ b. ■ c. ☐ d. ☐	3a. ☐ b. ☐ c. ☐ d. ■	3a. ☐ b. ■ c. ☐ d. ☐	3a. ☐ b. ☐ c. ■ d. ☐	3a. ☐ b. ☐ c. ■ d. ☐
4a. ■ b. ☐ c. ☐ d. ☐	4a. ☐ b. ■ c. ☐ d. ☐	4a. ☐ b. ☐ c. ☐ d. ■	4a. ☐ b. ☐ c. ☐ d. ■	4a. ☐ b. ☐ c. ■ d. ☐
5a. ☐ b. ☐ c. ■ d. ☐	5a. ☐ b. ☐ c. ■ d. ☐	5a. ■ b. ☐ c. ☐ d. ☐	5a. ☐ b. ☐ c. ☐ d. ■	5a. ☐ b. ■ c. ☐ d. ☐
6a. ☐ b. ■ c. ☐ d. ☐	6a. ☐ b. ☐ c. ☐ d. ■	6a. ☐ b. ☐ c. ☐ d. ■	6a. ■ b. ☐ c. ☐ d. ☐	6a. ☐ b. ☐ c. ■ d. ☐
7a. ☐ b. ☐ c. ☐ d. ■	7a. ☐ b. ■ c. ☐ d. ☐	7a. ☐ b. ■ c. ☐ d. ☐	7a. ☐ b. ■ c. ☐ d. ☐	7a. ■ b. ☐ c. ☐ d. ☐
8a. ☐ b. ☐ c. ■ d. ☐	8a. ■ b. ☐ c. ☐ d. ☐	8a. ☐ b. ☐ c. ■ d. ☐	8a. ☐ b. ☐ c. ■ d. ☐	8a. ☐ b. ☐ c. ☐ d. ■
9a. ☐ b. ☐ c. ☐ d. ■	9a. ☐ b. ■ c. ☐ d. ☐	9a. ☐ b. ■ c. ☐ d. ☐	9a. ■ b. ☐ c. ☐ d. ☐	9a. ☐ b. ■ c. ☐ d. ☐
10a. ☐ b. ■ c. ☐ d. ☐	10a. ■ b. ☐ c. ☐ d. ☐	10a. ☐ b. ■ c. ☐ d. ☐	10a. ☐ b. ☐ c. ☐ d. ■	10a. ☐ b. ☐ c. ■ d. ☐

801	802	803	804	805
1a. ☐	1a. ■	1a. ☐	1a. ☐	1a. ☐
b. ☐	b. ☐	b. ☐	b. ■	b. ☐
c. ■	c. ☐	c. ☐	c. ☐	c. ☐
d. ☐	d. ☐	d. ■	d. ☐	d. ■
2a. ☐	2a. ☐	2a. ■	2a. ☐	2a. ■
b. ■	b. ■	b. ☐	b. ■	b. ☐
c. ☐	c. ☐	c. ☐	c. ☐	c. ☐
d. ☐	d. ☐	d. ☐	d. ☐	d. ☐
3a. ■	3a. ☐	3a. ■	3a. ■	3a. ☐
b. ☐	b. ☐	b. ☐	b. ☐	b. ☐
c. ☐	c. ■	c. ☐	c. ☐	c. ■
d. ☐	d. ☐	d. ☐	d. ☐	d. ☐
4a. ☐	4a. ■	4a. ☐	4a. ☐	4a. ☐
b. ☐	b. ☐	b. ☐	b. ☐	b. ■
c. ☐	c. ☐	c. ■	c. ☐	c. ☐
d. ■	d. ☐	d. ☐	d. ■	d. ☐
5a. ☐	5a. ■	5a. ☐	5a. ☐	5a. ■
b. ☐	b. ☐	b. ■	b. ☐	b. ☐
c. ■	c. ☐	c. ☐	c. ■	c. ☐
d. ☐	d. ☐	d. ☐	d. ☐	d. ☐
6a. ☐	6a. ☐	6a. ■	6a. ☐	6a. ☐
b. ☐	b. ☐	b. ☐	b. ☐	b. ☐
c. ■	c. ☐	c. ☐	c. ☐	c. ☐
d. ☐	d. ■	d. ☐	d. ■	d. ■
7a. ■	7a. ■	7a. ☐	7a. ■	7a. ☐
b. ☐	b. ☐	b. ☐	b. ☐	b. ☐
c. ☐	c. ☐	c. ☐	c. ☐	c. ■
d. ☐	d. ☐	d. ■	d. ☐	d. ☐
8a. ☐	8a. ☐	8a. ☐	8a. ☐	8a. ☐
b. ■	b. ☐	b. ■	b. ☐	b. ■
c. ☐	c. ■	c. ☐	c. ☐	c. ☐
d. ☐	d. ☐	d. ☐	d. ■	d. ☐
9a. ☐	9a. ☐	9a. ☐	9a. ☐	9a. ☐
b. ■	b. ☐	b. ☐	b. ☐	b. ☐
c. ☐	c. ■	c. ■	c. ☐	c. ■
d. ☐	d. ☐	d. ☐	d. ■	d. ☐
10a. ☐	10a. ☐	10a. ☐	10a. ☐	10a. ☐
b. ☐	b. ■	b. ☐	b. ■	b. ☐
c. ☐	c. ☐	c. ■	c. ☐	c. ■
d. ■	d. ☐	d. ☐	d. ☐	d. ☐

#	806	807	808	809	810
1	a	a	b	a	b
2	d	c	a	d	d
3	d	c	b	d	c
4	c	b	d	c	c
5	a	d	c	d	a
6	c	b	b	c	b
7	b	c	d	a	d
8	d	a	d	c	d
9	b	d	b	a	b
10	c	b	b	c	c

Bible 200-800 Placement Worksheet

Student Name _____   Age _____

Date _____   Grade Last Completed

200	300	400	500	600	700	800
___	___	___	___	___	___	___
___	___	___	___	___	___	___
___	___	___	___	___	___	___
___	___	___	___	___	___	___
___	___	___	___	___	___	___
___	___	___	___	___	___	___
___	___	___	___	___	___	___
___	___	___	___	___	___	___
___	___	___	___	___	___	___
___	___	___	___	___	___	___

TOTAL ____   ____   ____   ____   ____   ____   ____
SCORE

GRADE LEVEL PLACEMENT: A student can be placed academically using the rule that he/she has successfully passed the test for any given level if he/she achieves a **Total Score of 70 points or more**.

This student places at grade level _____.

LEARNING GAPS: Learning gaps can be easily identified with the placement test. If a student receives **points of 6 or less** on any individual test, he/she has not shown mastery of the skills in that particular LIFEPAC. If desired, these LIFEPACs may be ordered and completed before the student begins his assigned grade level curriculum.

Learning gap LIFEPACs for this student are _____   _____   _____   _____

_____   _____   _____   _____

Note: It is not unusual for a student to place at more than one level in various subjects when beginning the LIFEPAC curriculum. For example, a student may be placed at 5th level in Bible, mathematics, science and history & geography but 4th level in language arts. The majority of school time should be concentrated on the areas of lower achievement with the ultimate goal of equal skill mastery in all subjects at the same grade level.

1. God's place for children to learn about the wisdom of God is in _____.
   a. church
   b. school
   c. the home
   d. a seminary

   1a. ☐
   b. ☐
   c. ☐
   d. ☐

2. The three worlds a person lives in are _____.
   a. earth, mars, moon
   b. play, work, sleep
   c. land, sea, city
   d. home, school, work

   2a. ☐
   b. ☐
   c. ☐
   d. ☐

3. Proverbs 1:10 advises that if sinners try to get you to go along with what they are doing you should _____.
   a. go along as a witness
   b. not consent
   c. pray for them
   d. tell on them

   3a. ☐
   b. ☐
   c. ☐
   d. ☐

4. Proverbs 3:5 and 6 tells us not to depend upon our own knowledge and wisdom, but to _____.
   a. ask advice from parents
   b. ask advice from a pastor
   c. ask advice from friends
   d. trust in the Lord in all our decisions

   4a. ☐
   b. ☐
   c. ☐
   d. ☐

5. Parents and children should _____ each other.
   a. correct
   b. listen to
   c. yell at
   d. ignore

   5a. ☐
   b. ☐
   c. ☐
   d. ☐

6. Children have a duty to _____ their parents.
   a. obey
   b. ignore
   c. change
   d. criticize

   6a. ☐
   b. ☐
   c. ☐
   d. ☐

7. Instead of hatred, jealousy, and bitterness, a Christian student should have _____.
   a. holiness
   b. generosity
   c. friendliness
   d. love

   7a. ☐
   b. ☐
   c. ☐
   d. ☐

8. At school a Christian should _____ non-Christians.
   a. show God's love to
   b. avoid
   c. become best friends with
   d. judge

   8a. ☐
   b. ☐
   c. ☐
   d. ☐

9. God wants His children to be industrious workers. *Industrious* means _____.
   a. being organized and not lazy
   b. working all the time
   c. doing anything to make a profit
   d. being greedy

   9a. ☐
   b. ☐
   c. ☐
   d. ☐

10. A Christian, in the world of work, should trust in God instead of in _____.
    a. knowledge
    b. riches
    c. the Holy Spirit
    d. the church

    10a. ☐
    b. ☐
    c. ☐
    d. ☐

1. In spite of criticism and opposition, the Bible _____.
    a. fights back
    b. continues to grow in influence and popularity
    c. disappears
    d. criticizes

2. The Bible must be God's Word because it has power to _____.
    a. cleanse and guide believers
    b. disappear
    c. be read
    d. exist

3. The Bible verse (Job 26:7) stating that, the earth "....hangeth upon nothing" refers to the forces of gravity and _____.
    a. energy
    b. antigravity
    c. inertia
    d. centrifugal force

4. In Isaiah 40:22 the prophet of God said that the Creator ". . . sitteth upon the circle of the earth . . . " Science has shown that the earth is _____.
    a. a sphere
    b. flat
    c. square
    d. a box

5. Evolutionists believe in the theory that life began _____.
    a. in the garden of Eden
    b. out in space
    c. in the ocean
    d. in the atmosphere

6. Evolutionists believe that the earth's atmosphere _____.
    a. has not changed
    b. has changed
    c. used to be poisonous
    d. could not support life at first

7. The Old Testament contains prophecies stating that _____.
    a. Christ would be raised from the dead
    b. Christ would not be raised from the dead
    c. the New Testament would be written
    d. the New Testament would not be written

8. The most important evidences for the Resurrection are _____.
    a. the signs in nature
    b. desires for it to be true
    c. the testimonies of those who saw Jesus after He arose
    d. The testimonies of angels

9. The church was established because of belief in _____.
    a. the Resurrection
    b. Christ's death
    c. Christ's ministry
    d. miracles

10. After the Resurrection Peter was _____.
    a. blind
    b. sad
    c. afraid
    d. transformed

. As a young man Paul was taught by _____.
  a. his parents
  b. one of the best Jewish teachers
  c. a Roman school
  d. Peter

1a. ☐
b. ☐
c. ☐
d. ☐

. Paul's conversion was unusual because he _____.
  a. could not remember
  b. became paralyzed
  c. was blinded
  d. could not speak

2a. ☐
b. ☐
c. ☐
d. ☐

. Most of Paul's letters were written to individual _____.
  a. churches
  b. people
  c. Jews
  d. missionaries

3a. ☐
b. ☐
c. ☐
d. ☐

. Paul placed the most importance on the _____ part of life.
  a. physical
  b. religious
  c. social
  d. spiritual

4a. ☐
b. ☐
c. ☐
d. ☐

. On his first missionary journey Paul first went to _____.
  a. Greece
  b. Cyprus
  c. Barnabas
  d. Sergius Paulus

5a. ☐
b. ☐
c. ☐
d. ☐

. In most cities where Paul preached, he established _____.
  a. Christian churches
  b. synagogues
  c. Bible schools
  d. retreats

6a. ☐
b. ☐
c. ☐
d. ☐

. On his second missionary journey Paul was accompanied by _____.
  a. no one
  b. Silas and Timothy
  c. Barnabas
  d. John Mark

7a. ☐
b. ☐
c. ☐
d. ☐

. On his second missionary journey Paul visited the churches he had established on his first journey and sailed to _____.
  a. Italy
  b. Greece
  c. Egypt
  d. Spain

8a. ☐
b. ☐
c. ☐
d. ☐

. Two people who helped Paul in Ephesus were _____.
  a. Priscilla and Aquila
  b. Lydia and Mary
  c. Mary and Martha
  d. Hannah and Sarah

9a. ☐
b. ☐
c. ☐
d. ☐

. First and Second Corinthians were written to the church at _____.
  a. Ephesus
  b. Corinth
  c. Antioch
  d. Jerusalem

10a. ☐
b. ☐
c. ☐
d. ☐

☐

1. Eternity begins for each person when _____ .
   a. the person dies
   b. God judges everyone
   c. the person is created
   d. the person is born again

   1a. ☐
   b. ☐
   c. ☐
   d. ☐

2. God gives eternal life to each person who _____ .
   a. goes to church
   b. worships God
   c. accepts Jesus as Saviour
   d. reads the Bible

   2a. ☐
   b. ☐
   c. ☐
   d. ☐

3. God wants each Christian to grow spiritually. Spiritual growth happens when a believer _____ God.
   a. obeys
   b. disobeys
   c. ignores
   d. thinks about

   3a. ☐
   b. ☐
   c. ☐
   d. ☐

4. A Christian should live a life separated from the world. A Christian _____ .
   a. should always be alone
   b. should never talk to an unsaved person
   c. should be totally committed to God
   d. cannot sin

   4a. ☐
   b. ☐
   c. ☐
   d. ☐

5. The judgment of believers is called _____ .
   a. the judgment seat of Christ
   b. the great white throne judgment
   c. Revelations
   d. the end times

   5a. ☐
   b. ☐
   c. ☐
   d. ☐

6. The purpose of the judgment of believers is to reveal the _____ of the deeds of each believer.
   a. salvation
   b. good deeds
   c. quality
   d. sins

   6a. ☐
   b. ☐
   c. ☐
   d. ☐

7. Those believers who endure temptation and obey God will receive the crown of _____ .
   a. life
   b. glory
   c. rejoicing
   d. eternity

   7a. ☐
   b. ☐
   c. ☐
   d. ☐

8. A crown of righteousness will be given to every Christian who _____ .
   a. dies before Christ comes
   b. loves the appearing of Christ
   c. never sins
   d. is a minister or missionary

   8a. ☐
   b. ☐
   c. ☐
   d. ☐

9. The judgment of the unsaved is called_____ .
   a. the judgment seat of Christ
   b. the great white throne judgment
   c. Revelations
   d. the end times

   9a. ☐
   b. ☐
   c. ☐
   d. ☐

10. The unsaved will spend eternity separated from _____ .
    a. God
    b. earth
    c. sin
    d. others

    10a. ☐
    b. ☐
    c. ☐
    d. ☐

. Natural laws are the _____.
   a. laws established by man   1a. ☐
   b. democratic laws   b. ☐
   c. forces which govern God's creation   c. ☐
   d. organic laws   d. ☐

.. The laws which govern man and his relationship to God are called_____.
   a. divine laws   2a. ☐
   b. natural laws   b. ☐
   c. Mosaic laws   c. ☐
   d. man's laws   d. ☐

. When Jesus came to earth as a man, he had the limitations of a man. Because of these limitations,
   Jesus was _____ just as we are.
   a. sinful   3a. ☐
   b. holy   b. ☐
   c. tempted   c. ☐
   d. disobedient   d. ☐

. For the believer the power to live God's way comes from God through _____.
   a. the Holy Spirit   4a. ☐
   b. the Scriptures   b. ☐
   c. the church   c. ☐
   d. laws   d. ☐

. God gives the authority in a family to _____.
   a. the church   5a. ☐
   b. the children   b. ☐
   c. the parent   c. ☐
   d. Christian teachers   d. ☐

. More freedom is usually the result of _____ to parents.
   a. disobedience   6a. ☐
   b. obedience   b. ☐
   c. talking back   c. ☐
   d. criticizing   d. ☐

. The first unit of government was _____.
   a. a tribe   7a. ☐
   b. Congress   b. ☐
   c. the church   c. ☐
   d. the family   d. ☐

. The basic laws during Moses' day were called _____.
   a. the Ten Commandments   8a. ☐
   b. laws of Israel   b. ☐
   c. Numbers   c. ☐
   d. democracy   d. ☐

. Government is responsible for _____.
   a. seeing that laws are carried out   9a. ☐
   b. making sure there is no freedom   b. ☐
   c. having a police force   c. ☐
   d. not changing   d. ☐

0. Two duties of citizens of the United States are to obey the laws and to _____.
   a. demonstrate   10a. ☐
   b. vote   b. ☐
   c. boycott   c. ☐
   d. go to church   d. ☐

☐

1. When Peter was in jail, an angel _____.
   a. came to release him
   b. stood outside and comforted him
   c. sang psalms to him
   d. killed the guards

   1a. [
   b. [
   c. [
   d. [

2. God is everywhere_____.
   a. at the same time
   b. every once in awhile
   c. sometime
   d. only when you pray

   2a. [
   b. [
   c. [
   d. [

3. The man who had tuberculosis and spent his short life taking the message of Christ to the American Indians was _____.
   a. David Livingstone
   b. David Brainerd
   c. George Washington
   d. Benjamin Franklin

   3a. [
   b. [
   c. [
   d. [

4. Parents have a duty to _____ their children.
   a. correct
   b. yell at
   c. ignore
   d. change

   4a. [
   b. [
   c. [
   d. [

5. The judge at the judgment of believers will be _____.
   a. the Holy Spirit
   b. the angels
   c. Moses
   d. Christ

   5a. [
   b. [
   c. [
   d. [

6. The heavenly rewards Christians will receive will _____.
   a. last for eternity
   b. be temporary
   c. be given by angels
   d. bring honor to the Christians

   6a. [
   b. [
   c. [
   d. [

7. God is the source of all law and authority because he is _____.
   a. holy
   b. the creator
   c. God
   d. a, b, and c

   7a. [
   b. [
   c. [
   d. [

8. Keeping your room clean is one way you can show _____ to your parents.
   a. disrespect
   b. honor
   c. fear
   d. disobedience

   8a. [
   b. [
   c. [
   d. [

9. Government is needed to maintain order. Lack of order leads to _____.
   a. prosperity
   b. long lines
   c. health and safety hazards
   d. fair standards

   9a. [
   b. [
   c. [
   d. [

10. Christians need to _____ for the government.
    a. rejoice
    b. mourn
    c. sacrifice
    d. pray

    10a. [
    b. [
    c. [
    d. [

On the first day God created _____.
  a. light
  b. water creatures
  c. man
  d. trees

1a. ☐
b. ☐
c. ☐
d. ☐

God breathed into man the breath of life and man became a living _____.
  a. person
  b. soul
  c. spirit
  d. animal

2a. ☐
b. ☐
c. ☐
d. ☐

The man chosen to build the ark was_____.
  a. Abraham
  b. Adam
  c. Ham
  d. Noah

3a. ☐
b. ☐
c. ☐
d. ☐

The man who had a special experience at Peniel, which means the face of God, was _____.
  a. Joseph
  b. Jacob
  c. Esau
  d. Abraham

4a. ☐
b. ☐
c. ☐
d. ☐

God spoke to _____ out of the burning bush.
  a. Moses
  b. Abraham
  c. Joseph
  d. Isaac

5a. ☐
b. ☐
c. ☐
d. ☐

The book which follows Leviticus is _____.
  a. Deuteronomy
  b. Numbers
  c. Genesis
  d. Proverbs

6a. ☐
b. ☐
c. ☐
d. ☐

God led His people, Israel, during the day with _____.
  a. a cloud
  b. a pillar of fire
  c. angels
  d. a strong wind

7a. ☐
b. ☐
c. ☐
d. ☐

During the night God led His people, Israel, with _____.
  a. a cloud
  b. a pillar of fire
  c. angels
  d. a strong wind

8a. ☐
b. ☐
c. ☐
d. ☐

Of all the spies sent to Canaan, _____ were willing to believe God's promise to give them the land.
  a. all
  b. only two
  c. none
  d. ten

9a. ☐
b. ☐
c. ☐
d. ☐

The children of Israel _____.
  a. never arrived in the Promised Land
  b. finally went into the Promised Land after the forty years in the wilderness
  c. returned to Egypt
  d. never doubted God again

10a. ☐
b. ☐
c. ☐
d. ☐

1. Israel suffered defeat at Ai because_____.
    a. of sin among the Israelites
    b. Ai had a more powerful army
    c. Israel was not prepared for battle
    d. the people of Ai obeyed God

2. God gave an inheritance of land to _____.
    a. each individual
    b. to each tribe except Levi
    c. the tribe of Levi
    d. only half of the tribes

3. The only woman judge over Israel was _____.
    a. Ruth
    b. Naomi
    c. Deborah
    d. Mary

4. A judge who was known for his great strength and for the deliverance of Israel from the Philistines was _____.
    a. Gideon
    b. Samson
    c. Samuel
    d. Eglon

5. After Joshua's death what did Israel do to the Canaanites?
    a. killed all of them
    b. did not drive them all out of the land
    c. converted them
    d. drove them all out of the land

6. During the period of the judges, the Israelites behaved the same way over and over again. The Israelites would sin, then repent. God would send a judge to deliver them. A period of _____ would follow. Then the Israelites would sin again.
    a. punishment
    b. judging
    c. disobedience
    d. blessing and peace

7. God's love for Ruth was shown by _____.
    a. Orpah's love
    b. Ruth's love
    c. many riches
    d. a new home

8. Ruth loved and married _____.
    a. Obed
    b. David
    c. Boaz
    d. Samuel

9. The book which is *not* one of the twelve Old Testament books of history is _____.
    a. Joshua
    b. Judges
    c. Ruth
    d. Song of Solomon

10. The books which are *not* part of the twelve Old Testament books of history are _____.
    a. First and Second Samuel
    b. First and Second Kings
    c. Job and Obadiah
    d. First and Second Chronicles

1a. [
  b. [
  c. [
  d. [

2a. [
  b. [
  c. [
  d. [

3a. [
  b. [
  c. [
  d. [

4a.
  b.
  c.
  d.

5a.
  b.
  c.
  d.

6a.
  b.
  c.
  d.

7a.
  b.
  c.
  d.

8a.
  b.
  c.
  d.

9a.
  b.
  c.
  d.

10a.
  b.
  c.
  d.

Saul began to lose God's favor when he _____.
a. spared Agag
b. ordered a feast
c. became impatient and offered a sacrifice
d. became proud of his victories

1a. ☐
b. ☐
c. ☐
d. ☐

"The house" which God promised to David was _____.
a. a royal family through Jesus Christ
b. a beautiful palace
c. a temple for Israel to worship in
d. a capital city for Israel

2a. ☐
b. ☐
.c. ☐
d. ☐

During Solomon's reign the _____ was built.
a. Ark
b. Tabernacle
c. Temple
d. Palace

3a. ☐
b. ☐
c. ☐
d. ☐

Solomon also built many _____.
a. cities
b. fortresses
c. buildings
d. a, b, and c

4a. ☐
b. ☐
c. ☐
d. ☐

When Solomon became king, he asked God for _____.
a. wisdom
b. wealth
c. power
d. success

5a. ☐
b. ☐
c. ☐
d. ☐

God blessed Solomon with great _____.
a. health
b. wealth
c. strength
d. musical abilities

6a. ☐
b. ☐
c. ☐
d. ☐

Most of the Proverbs were written by _____.
a. David
b. Job
c. Saul
d. Solomon

7a. ☐
b. ☐
c. ☐
d. ☐

Most of the Psalms were written by _____.
a. David
b. Job
c. Saul
d. Solomon

8a. ☐
b. ☐
c. ☐
d. ☐

The three types of Psalms are instructional, historical, and _____.
a. musical
b. prophetical
c. glorifying
d. thankful

9a. ☐
b. ☐
c. ☐
d. ☐

The theme of Song of Solomon is _____.
a. love
b. forgiveness
c. wisdom
d. grace

10a. ☐
b. ☐
c. ☐
d. ☐

1. Judah, the southern kingdom, was made up of _____ tribes.
   a. two
   b. ten
   c. twelve
   d. eight

2. Solomon's son who became king of Judah was _____.
   a. Jereboam
   b. Elijah
   c. Asa
   d. Rehoboam

3. Jehosophat was a king of Judah who _____.
   a. worshiped Baal
   b. fought many wars against Israel
   c. walked in the ways of the Lord
   d. tried to capture the kingdom of Israel

4. The kings and the people of Israel _____.
   a. disobeyed God and worshiped false gods
   b. became a powerful and wealthy kingdom
   c. obeyed the voice of God
   d. repented of their sins

5. The prophet who called upon God to send fire to burn his sacrifice was _____.
   a. Jonah
   b. Elisha
   c. Daniel
   d. Elijah

6. Amos called upon the people of Israel to repent and to demonstrate the fruit of repentance, which is _____.
   a. righteousness
   b. forgiveness
   c. religion
   d. feeling sorry

7. Josiah became king of Judah when he was eight years old and he _____.
   a. destroyed the Temple
   b. was a wicked king
   c. was cruel to the people
   d. did what was right in the sight of the Lord

8. Judah was finally taken into captivity by _____.
   a. Assyria
   b. Egypt
   c. Babylon
   d. Rome

9. The promise of a Messiah born to a virgin was included in God's message to Ahaz by the prophet_____.
   a. Isaiah
   b. Jonah
   c. Micah
   d. Habakkuk

10. The prophet who was a major prophet is _____.
   a. Amos
   b. Jeremiah
   c. Mijcah
   d. Nahum

604
1a.
b.
c.
d.

2a.
b.
c.
d.

3a.
b.
c.
d.

4a.
b.
c.
d.

5a.
b.
c.
d.

6a.
b.
c.
d.

7a.
b.
c.
d.

8a.
b.
c.
d.

9a.
b.
c.
d.

10a.
b.
c.
d.

The three prophets to Judah during the Babylonian Captivity were Jeremiah, Ezekiel, and
_____.

a. Daniel
b. Isaiah
c. Jonah
d. Esther

1a. ☐
b. ☐
c. ☐
d. ☐

Because Daniel continued to pray to and worship God in spite of a decree by the government,
he_____.
a. was put into a fiery furnace
b. lost his high position in government
c. was thrown into the lions' den
d. was imprisoned in Babylon

2a. ☐
b. ☐
c. ☐
d. ☐

Nehemiah received permission to return to Palestine from King _____.
a. Artaxerxes
b. Nebuchadnezzar
c. Xerxes
d. Babylon

3a. ☐
b. ☐
c. ☐
d. ☐

The three returns from exile were led by Zerubbabel, Ezra, and _____.
a. Isaiah
b. Mordecai
c. Nehemiah
d. Daniel

4a. ☐
b. ☐
c. ☐
d. ☐

During the first return under Zerubbabel, the Temple was_____.
a. destroyed
b. half finished
c. renamed
d. rebuilt

5a. ☐
b. ☐
c. ☐
d. ☐

Nehemiah helped the people _____.
a. rebuild the Temple
b. rebuild the walls of Jerusalem
c. repent
d. wanting to return to Babylon

6a. ☐
b. ☐
c. ☐
d. ☐

Esther was _____.
a. a Gentile
b. a Jew
c. a Babylonian
d. an Assyrian

7a. ☐
b. ☐
c. ☐
d. ☐

Haman wanted to have _____.
a. all the Jews destroyed
b. the throne taken away from King Ahasuerus
c. Esther made Queen
d. the Jews returned to Palestine

8a. ☐
b. ☐
c. ☐
d. ☐

Haggai and Zechariah both spoke to Israel about _____.
a. Babylon
b. defending Jerusalem
c. worship and the condition of the Temple
d. restoring the land

9a. ☐
b. ☐
c. ☐
d. ☐

Zechariah also prophesied about the _____.
a. next captivity
b. downfall of the Jews
c. Antichrist
d. Messiah

10a. ☐
b. ☐
c. ☐
d. ☐

☐

1. The four books of the new Testament that give the story of Christ's life are _____.
   a. Matthew, Mark, Luke, and John
   b. Acts, Romans, First Corinthians, and Second Corinthians
   c. Galatians, Ephesians, Philippians, and Colossians
   d. Hebrews, James, First Peter, and Second Peter

2. Jesus fed a crowd of five thousand people with only _____.
   a. one loaf of bread
   b. five loaves of bread and two fishes
   c. three jugs of water
   d. five fishes

3. On the Cross, Jesus experienced both physical pain and great _____ suffering for our sins.
   a. spiritual
   b. physical
   c. invisible
   d. emotional

4. Jesus died on the Cross and arose from the dead in order that _____.
   a. God could perform another miracle
   b. He could return to heaven
   c. man might be saved from sin
   d. the Roman Empire might be defeated

5. Jesus told the rich young ruler he needed to _____.
   a. sell all he had and bring the money to Jesus
   b. sell all he had and give it to the priests
   c. sell all he had and give it to the poor
   d. make more money and give it to the poor

6. The parable of the prodigal son illustrates that the heavenly Father is _____.
   a. happy when a person repents
   b. not expecting anyone to repent
   c. slow to forgive when someone repents
   d. expecting us to sin

7 The Old Testament prophesied that Jesus would be born in _____.
   a. Bethlehem
   b. Nazareth
   c. Judah
   d. Egypt

8. Isaiah also described the ministry of _____.
   a. the disciples
   b. Jesus
   c. the church
   d. the Apostles

9. Hebrews 13:8 says, "Jesus Christ the same _____."
   a. yesterday, and today, and forever
   b. always
   c. for eternity
   d. to everyone

10. John 1:1 says, " In the beginning was the Word, and the Word was with God, and the Word was God." "The Word" refers to _____.
   a. the Bible
   b. the Mosaic Law
   c. God's voice
   d. Jesus

1a. [
b. [
c. [
d. [

2a. [
b. [
c. [
d. [

3a. [
b. [
c. [
d. [

4a. [
b. [
c. [
d. [

5a. [
b. [
c. [
d. [

6a. [
b. [
c. [
d. [

7a. [
b. [
c. [
d. [

8a. [
b. [
c. [
d. [

9a. [
b. [
c. [
d. [

10a. [
b. [
c. [
d. [

1. The person who was *not* a disciple is _____.
   a. Peter
   b. James
   c. John
   d. Joseph

2. The person who was *not* a disciple is _____.
   a. Thomas
   b. Matthew
   c. Barnabas
   d. James

3. Jesus' message to Nicodemus was that a person must be _____.
   a. willing to do good works
   b. born again
   c. holy
   d. sinless

4. Salvation comes through faith in _____.
   a. Christ
   b. church
   c. religion
   d. good works

5. Martha had to learn that _____ matters were more important than other things.
   a. spiritual
   b. daily
   c. physical
   d. expensive

6. Jesus taught Martha that those who believe in Him will never die _____.
   a. physically
   b. at all
   c. painfully
   d. spiritually

7. Jesus healed the centurion's servant because _____.
   a. the centurion had built a synagogue
   b. the centurion had faith in Christ
   c. the centurion deserved a favor
   d. Jesus wanted the servant to become a disciple

8. After Jesus healed the demoniac, people were amazed to see this man _____.
   a. going to church
   b. feeding the poor
   c. sitting quietly and listening to Jesus
   d. preaching the gospel

9. A woman who had been sick for twelve years was healed when she touched Jesus' _____.
   a. hand
   b. garment
   c. disciples
   d. footprint

10. Ten lepers were healed by Jesus because of their _____.
    a. disease
    b. sorrow
    c. joy
    d. faith

47

1. As a child Paul was taught much about _____.
   a. religion and the Bible
   b. astronomy
   c. science
   d. medicine

1a. [
  b. [
  c. [
  d. [

2. Paul accepted Christ after seeing a light from heaven and hearing _____.
   a. angels singing
   b. Abraham
   c. the voice of Jesus
   d. the cries of Christians

2a. [
  b. [
  c. [
  d. [

3. Paul and Silas were imprisoned on the second missionary journey. Because they did not escape after the earthquake opened the gates, the jailer _____.
   a. was saved
   b. killed himself
   c. killed Paul and Silas
   d. punished Paul and Silas

3a. [
  b. [
  c. [
  d. [

4. After his third journey Paul wanted to return to Jerusalem to _____.
   a. celebrate the feast of Pentecost
   b. preach to the Jews
   c. rest and relax
   d. visit his family

4a. [
  b. [
  c. [
  d. [

5. Paul's arrival in Rome was delayed by _____.
   a. sickness
   b. weariness
   c. friends
   d. a storm at sea

5a. [
  b. [
  c. [
  d. [

6. In Rome Paul ministered to _____.
   a. only the Jews
   b. only the Gentiles
   c. both the Jews and Gentiles
   d. only prisoners

6a. [
  b. [
  c. [
  d. [

7. The book which was *not* written by Paul is _____.
   a. Romans
   b. First Corinthians
   c. Galatians
   d. Acts

7a. [
  b. [
  c. [
  d. [

8. The book which was *not* written by Paul is _____.
   a. First Thessalonians
   b. Second Timothy
   c. James
   d. Titus

8a. [
  b. [
  c. [
  d. [

9. Paul reminded the Ephesians that salvation is by grace, through faith, not of_____.
   a. sins
   b. favor
   c. works
   d. heritage

9a. [
  b. [
  c. [
  d. [

10. The book of Romans was written _____ Paul's stay in Rome.
    a. before
    b. during
    c. after
    d. in spite of

10a. [
   b. [
   c. [
   d. [

The writer of the Epistle to the Hebrews wanted to prevent his readers from _____.
a. studying the Old Testament
b. forgetting the Old Testament
c. being persecuted
d. going back to Judaism

The writer tried to accomplish his purpose by proving to them that _____.
a. Judaism had come to an end in Christ
b. Jesus had come to earth
c. Joshua was better than Moses
d. a church was better than a synagogue

2a. ☐
b. ☐
c. ☐
d. ☐

The theme of the Epistle to the Hebrews is _____.
a. Moses was superior to Abraham
b. the Christian faith is superior to Judaism
c. prophets were superior to angels
d. the apostles were superior to the prophets

3a. ☐
b. ☐
c. ☐
d. ☐

A comparative word that is used thirteen times in the Epistle to the Hebrews is _____.
a. *worse*
b. *better*
c. *older*
d. *newer*

4a. ☐
b. ☐
c. ☐
d. ☐

Paul is the author of _____.
a. Jude
b. James
c. Thomas
d. none of these

5a. ☐
b. ☐
c. ☐
d. ☐

Of the seven General Epistles the two that were addressed to individuals are _____.
a. First and Second John
b. Second and Third John
c. First and Second Peter
d. James and Jude

6a. ☐
b. ☐
c. ☐
d. ☐

Epistles that warned against false teachers were Second Peter, First John, Jude and _____.
a. Second John
b. First Peter
c. Third John
d. James

7a. ☐
b. ☐
c. ☐
d. ☐

Peter stated two purposes in writing his first Epistle. They were to exhort and to _____.
a. testify
b. judge
c. scold
d. warn

8a. ☐
b. ☐
c. ☐
d. ☐

The truths Peter taught in his second Epistle are provision for a holy life and _____.
a. divine inspiration of the Holy Word
b. warning against false teachers within the church
c. the promise of Christ's coming
d. a, b, and c

9a. ☐
b. ☐
c. ☐
d. ☐

In his second Epistle John warned the elect lady against false teachers who _____.
a. denied the Old Testament
b. denied that Jesus had come in the flesh
c. taught the need for circumcision
d. taught that it was wrong to eat meat

10a. ☐
b. ☐
c. ☐
d. ☐

1. The seventh day of Creation was a day of _____ .
   a. celebration
   b. work
   c. rest
   d. introduction

2. The first book of the Bible is _____ .
   a. Matthew
   b. Deuteronomy
   c. Genesis
   d. Proverbs

3. The book which is *not* one of the first five books of the Bible is _____.
   a. Genesis
   b. Deuteronomy
   c. Esther
   d. Numbers

4. The book which is *not* one of the twelve Old Testament books of history is _____ .
   a. Ezekiel
   b. Ezra
   c. Nehemiah
   d. Esther

5. The Lord took away His blessing from Solomon because he _____.
   a. died
   b. married many wives and turned away from God
   c. became too old to rule
   d. murdered Jeroboam

6. The kingdom of Israel ended when _____.
   a. the kingdom of Judah defeated it
   b. God united Judah and Israel again
   c. the Assyrians took Israel captive
   d. everyone died

7. Jesus raised Lazarus from the dead. One of the results of this miracle was that _____.
   a. Lazarus never died
   b. many people believed in Jesus
   c. the religious leaders believed in Jesus
   d. some disciples left in fear

8. The number of lepers who returned to thank Jesus was _____ .
   a. ten
   b. nine
   c. one
   d. five

9. The book which was *not* written by Paul is _____.
   a. Ephesians
   b. Jude
   c. Philippians
   d. Colossians

10. The four Epistles written during Paul's time in prison in Rome are Ephesians, Philippians, Colossians, and _____ .
   a. Romans
   b. Philemon
   c. First Timothy
   d. Titus

610

1a.
b.
c.
d.

2a.
b.
c.
d.

3a.
b.
c.
d.

4a.
b.
c.
d.

5a.
b.
c.
d.

6a.
b.
c.
d.

7a.
b.
c.
d.

8a.
b.
c.
d.

9a.
b.
c.
d.

10a.
b.
c.
d.

The most common Old Testament word(s) used for *worship* is to _____.
a. *serve*
b. *adore*
c. *bow down*
d. *sacrifice*

1a. ☐
b. ☐
c. ☐
d. ☐

The early Christians worshiped God in the _____.
a. Temple
b. church
c. synagogue
d. a, b, and c

2a. ☐
b. ☐
c. ☐
d. ☐

True worship involves worshiping God the _____.
a. Father
b. Son
c. Holy Spirit
d. truth

3a. ☐
b. ☐
c. ☐
d. ☐

The way to approach the true God in worship is through _____.
a. prayer
b. Jesus
c. kneeling
d. sacrifice

4a. ☐
b. ☐
c. ☐
d. ☐

A person who worships God outwardly but who inwardly has no love for God is a(n) _____.
a. hypocrite
b. idolater
c. pagan
d. atheist

5a. ☐
b. ☐
c. ☐
d. ☐

Going through the motions of worship when your heart is not in it is called _____.
a. idolatry
b. hypocrisy
c. formalism
d. atheism

6a. ☐
b. ☐
c. ☐
d. ☐

We should worship God because He is _____.
a. a jealous God
b. a vengeful God
c. the Creator
d. the Father of Jesus

7a. ☐
b. ☐
c. ☐
d. ☐

Our worship of God is recognition of His _____.
a. origin
b. universe
c. terror
d. worth

8a. ☐
b. ☐
c. ☐
d. ☐

The Scriptures teach that Christians are not to _____.
a. worship on Saturday
b. pray quietly
c. forsake coming together
d. bear another's burdens

9a. ☐
b. ☐
c. ☐
d. ☐

The worship of God brings _____.
a. fullness of joy
b. salvation
c. unification
d. repentance

10a. ☐
b. ☐
c. ☐
d. ☐

☐

1. The method God used to bring man into existence was _____.
   a. mutation
   b. evolution
   c. Creation
   d. spontaneous

2. The fist aspect of man to come into existence was his _____.
   a. soul
   b. body
   c. spirit
   d. mind

3. As shown by Jesus Christ, man is to worship God and to _____.
   a. offer sacrifices
   b. preach
   c. serve Him
   d. learn about God

4. Man bears the image of _____.
   a. God
   b. man
   c. woman
   d. earth

5. The first human to sin was _____.
   a. Adam
   b. Eve
   c. Cain
   d. Satan

6. The one who is responsible for sin in a person's life is _____.
   a. Adam
   b. the person himself
   c. no one
   d. Cain

7. A person can experience forgiveness of sins through _____.
   a. penance
   b. self-sacrifice
   c. meritorious service
   d. Christ's sacrifice

8. The word used to refer to God buying man back from sin is _____.
   a. propitiation
   b. impute
   c. redeem
   d. sacrifice

9. Christians are known by their _____.
   a. church
   b. love
   c. dress
   d. speech

10. Man is required to do justly, to love kindness, and to _____.
    a. go to church
    b. be poor
    c. walk humbly with God
    d. show good leadership

Because man is sinful and needs help, God extends His _____.

a. love
b. mercy
c. grace
d. justice

1a. ☐
b. ☐
c. ☐
d. ☐

God's nature can be defined as _____.
a. love
b. mercy
c. grace
d. justice

2a. ☐
b. ☐
c. ☐
d. ☐

God expresses His love by _____.
a. making the world
b. making man
c. giving His Son
d. giving the Bible

3a. ☐
b. ☐
c. ☐
d. ☐

God shows mercy by _____.
a. forfeiting love
b. feeling sorrow
c. forgetting justice
d. forgiving sinners

4a. ☐
b. ☐
c. ☐
d. ☐

God's love for you _____.
a. depends on your behavior
b. can cease
c. never changes
d. is variable

5a. ☐
b. ☐
c. ☐
d. ☐

We love God because He _____.
a. blesses us
b. is so good
c. loved us first
d. does not change

6a. ☐
b. ☐
c. ☐
d. ☐

When Jesus took the punishment of sin, God was showing His _____.
a. anger
b. mercy
c. justice
d. eternity

7a. ☐
b. ☐
c. ☐
d. ☐

God shows His mercy by sending rain on _____.
a. the just and the unjust
b. the desert
c. His children
d. watersheds

8a. ☐
b. ☐
c. ☐
d. ☐

God's grace is _____.
a. expensive
b. earned
c. free
d. unnecessary

9a. ☐
b. ☐
c. ☐
d. ☐

The word *grace* means _____.
a. *generous favor*
b. *unmerited favor*
c. *merited favor*
d. *limited favor*

10a. ☐
b. ☐
c. ☐
d. ☐

☐

1. The first prophecy of the coming Messiah refers to Him as the _____.
   a. Messiah
   b. Branch
   c. Tree of Life
   d. seed of the woman

2. The Messiah would give light because He was the star of _____.
   a. heaven
   b. Jacob
   c. Adam
   d. God

3. The primary purpose of Christ's first Advent was to _____.
   a. be a good example
   b. make disciples
   c. teach people about God
   d. be a sacrifice for sin

4. Something that symbolized Jesus that the Israelites looked to for healing was _____.
   a. Moses' rod
   b. Aaron's breastplate
   c. the Tabernacle
   d. a brass serpent

5. As a King and as a Refuge, Jesus fulfills the office of _____.
   a. President
   b. Servant
   c. Governor
   d. Lamb

6. The length of time that Jesus would be in the grave was fore-told in the book of _____.
   a. Numbers
   b. Malachi
   c. Jonah
   d. Revelation

7. Jesus' prophesied Resurrection was fulfilled according to _____.
   a. Matthew 5:1
   b. Matthew 16:7
   c. Matthew 1:18
   d. Matthew 28:6

8. Jesus called the cup at the Last Supper His blood of the _____.
   a. grape
   b. marriage wine
   c. New Testament
   d. Resurrection

9. The historical evidence of the authenticity of Biblical prophecy is _____.
   a. its fulfillment
   b. its author
   c. earlier prophecies
   d. earlier history

10. Prophecy is a declaration of knowledge that belongs exclusively to _____.
   a. Israel
   b. God
   c. the prophet
   d. mankind

1a. [
b. [
c. [
d. [

2a. [
b. [
c. [
d. [

3a. [
b. [
c. [
d. [

4a.
b.
c.
d.

5a.
b.
c.
d.

6a.
b.
c.
d.

7a.
b.
c.
d.

8a.
b.
c.
d.

9a.
b.
c.
d.

10a.
b.
c.
d.

The person who has only natural, human life is motivated _____.

a. to do good
b. to please God
c. by the Bible
d. by the sin nature

1a. ☐
b. ☐
c. ☐
d. ☐

A person becomes spiritually alive when he _____.

a. is born
b. trusts Christ
c. dies
d. learns of God

2a. ☐
b. ☐
c. ☐
d. ☐

Although morality is important, it should never be _____.

a. our standard for pleasing God
b. a part of our lives
c. used in the world
d. used by Christians

3a. ☐
b. ☐
c. ☐
d. ☐

The sinner can be deceived into thinking his sins _____.

a. can be forgiven
b. are known by God
c. are too great
d. will be judged

4a. ☐
b. ☐
c. ☐
d. ☐

The way to be forgiven of our sins is to _____.

a. protect them
b. hide them
c. forget them
d. confess them

5a. ☐
b. ☐
c. ☐
d. ☐

In Matthew 4:4 Jesus said that God's Word is as important as _____.

a. meat
b. bread
c. water
d. gold

6a. ☐
b. ☐
c. ☐
d. ☐

As God's children we should _____.

a. please ourselves
b. always feel guilty
c. love the world
d. imitate Christ

7a. ☐
b. ☐
c. ☐
d. ☐

The goal for the Christian is that He _____.

a. win the world for Christ
b. mature in Christ
c. eat the milk of the Word
d. become a Jew

8a. ☐
b. ☐
c. ☐
d. ☐

God's desire is for the Christian to do all things _____.

a. unto the Lord
b. before Christ's return
c. with other Christians
d. with solemnity

9a. ☐
b. ☐
c. ☐
d. ☐

Faith, meekness, and temperance are items of the fruit of the Spirit directed toward _____.

a. God
b. parents
c. self
d. others

10a. ☐
b. ☐
c. ☐
d. ☐

☐

1. The Hebrew title of the Psalms is *tehillim* and means _____.
   a. *song*
   b. *praise*
   c. *poetry*
   d. *noise*

2. The book of Psalms contains Psalms written by at least _____.
   a. twenty-three men
   b. four Egyptians
   c. five women
   d. seven men

3. The Psalms comment on almost every area of _____.
   a. devotion
   b. theology
   c. history
   d. ethics

4. For over two thousand years, Psalm 92 has been read on every Jewish _____ day.
   a. Sabbath
   b. festival
   c. fast
   d. harvest

5. English poetry rhymes *sounds,* but Hebrew poetry rhymes _____.
   a. letters
   b. lines
   c. ideas
   d. words

6. "They are brought down and fallen: but we are risen, and stand upright" is an example of _____ parallelism.
   a. synthetic
   b. antithetical
   c. synonymous
   d. emblematic

7. The pattern to guide the singing of some psalms cannot be determined because of the structure of _____.
   a. the stringed instruments
   b. the book of Psalms
   c. Hebrew poetry
   d. the Hebrew language

8. The word *psalm* refers to _____.
   a. a title of a poem
   b. a stringed instrument
   c. a song sung with instruments
   d. pattern or meter

9. The author of Psalm 100 is _____.
   a. David
   b. Solomon
   c. Asaph
   d. unknown

10. The major theological theme of Psalm 100 concerns man's relationship with _____.
    a. man
    b. God
    c. the world
    d. the Bible

The person who did not know before His birth that Jesus was the Messiah was _____.

a. Gabriel
b. Elisabeth
c. Anna
d. Mary

Jesus grew up in the city of _____.

a. Nazareth
b. Jerusalem
c. Bethlehem
d. Galilee

2a. ☐
b. ☐
c. ☐
d. ☐

Jesus was baptized as a sign of His _____.

a. repentance
b. priesthood
c. mission to man
d. submission to God

3a. ☐
b. ☐
c. ☐
d. ☐

Satan tempted Jesus in _____.

a. the garden of Gethseurane
b. three areas of life
c. the Tabernacle
d. nine points of theology

4a. ☐
b. ☐
c. ☐
d. ☐

The disciples became Apostles after they were _____.

a. dead
b. baptized
c. commissioned
d. called

5a. ☐
b. ☐
c. ☐
d. ☐

All of the disciples were from Galilee except _____.

a. Judas
b. Simon
c. Thaddeaus
d. Bartholomew

6a. ☐
b. ☐
c. ☐
d. ☐

Jesus told Nicodemus that he had to be born of water and of the _____.

a. flesh
b. Spirit
c. Law
d. Gospel

7a. ☐
b. ☐
c. ☐
d. ☐

The Samaritan woman gave evidence of being very _____.

a. intelligent
b. thirsty
c. religious
d. righteous

8a. ☐
b. ☐
c. ☐
d. ☐

In His sermon in Jerusalem, Jesus said that John, God, and the Scriptures _____.

a. strengthened Him
b. bore witness of Him
c. were eternal.
d. were holy

9a. ☐
b. ☐
c. ☐
d. ☐

In His Sermon on the mount, Jesus stressed the inner spirit of _____.

a. the Law
b. man
c. God
d. the Scriptures

10a. ☐
b. ☐
c. ☐
d. ☐

1. Jesus' miracles revealed His _____.
   a. power
   b. authority
   c. compassion
   d. a, b, and c

2. The feeding of the five thousand illustrated that Jesus is _____.
   a. the Messiah
   b. compassionate
   c. the Bread of Life
   d. a servant of man

3. One of the main reasons Jesus began to use parables was _____.
   a. to make His message clear
   b. the peoples' disbelief
   c. to extend His ministry
   d. the clarity of parables

4. Parables required the listener to _____.
   a. study the Scriptures
   b. forget the truth
   c. ask their meaning
   d. interpret their meaning

5. Jesus taught divine truth to His disciples by almost _____ of His miracles.
   a. one-third
   b. all
   c. one-half
   d. three-fourth

6. Jesus prepared His disciples for ministry by sending them _____.
   a. out to fish
   b. to the desert
   c. to the school of the prophets
   d. to preach and to heal

7. The two men who appeared at Jesus' Transfiguration were _____.
   a. Moses and Elisha
   b. Moses and Elijah
   c. Moses and Adam
   d. Elisha and David

8. The disciples who witnessed the Transfiguration were _____.
   a. John, Thomas, and James
   b. James, Judas, and Simon
   c. Peter, James, and John
   d. Judas, John, and James

9. Jesus' later Judean ministry could be called a ministry of _____.
   a. miracles
   b. conflict
   c. destruction
   d. cleansing

10. In Perea Jesus healed a blind man named _____.
    a. Lazarus
    b. Bartimaeus
    c. Zacchaeus
    d. Barjesus

To the shouts of "Hosanna," Jesus entered _____.
a. Jerusalem
b. Nazareth
c. Bethlehem
d. Capernaum

Jesus said that the Temple should not be a den of thieves but a house of _____.
a. sacrifice
b. singing
c. prayer
d. learning

The last Jewish feast that Jesus shared with His disciples was the feast of_____.
a. first fruits
b. Trumpets
c. Passover
d. Tabernacles

After the Last Supper, Jesus _____.
a. left the disciples
b. washed the disciples' feet
c. fell asleep
d. walked with His disciples

Before His Crucifixion, Jesus endured _____ trials.
a. three
b. four
c. five
d. six

The charge brought against Jesus was _____.
a. blasphemy
b. lying
c. treason
d. insanity

Golgotha is also known as the place of _____.
a. death
b. a skull
c. judgment
d. the Cross

When Jesus died, there occurred a great _____.
a. noise
b. light
c. earthquake
d. flood

Jesus had to rise from the dead because He _____.
a. is God
b. loved His disciples
c. had more to teach
d. sent the Spirit

Through the Ascension, Jesus has become the believer's _____.
a. sacrifice
b. teacher
c. brother
d. mediator

1a. ☐
b. ☐
c. ☐
d. ☐

2a. ☐
b. ☐
c. ☐
d. ☐

3a. ☐
b. ☐
c. ☐
d. ☐

4a. ☐
b. ☐
c. ☐
d. ☐

5a. ☐
b. ☐
c. ☐
d. ☐

6a. ☐
b. ☐
c. ☐
d. ☐

7a. ☐
b. ☐
c. ☐
d. ☐

8a. ☐
b. ☐
c. ☐
d. ☐

9a. ☐
b. ☐
c. ☐
d. ☐

10a. ☐
b. ☐
c. ☐
d. ☐

1. Because man is guilty, God extends His _____.
   a. love
   b. mercy
   c. grace
   d. justice

2. Grace and truth came to man by _____.
   a. Jesus Christ
   b. Moses
   c. the Bible
   d. Creation

3. Isaiah 7:14 says that the Messiah would be born _____.
   a. in a manger
   b. in Bethlehem
   c. of a virgin
   d. in Israel

4. The office of Christ associated with suffering and death is that of _____.
   a. Prophet
   b. King
   c. Redeemer
   d. Priest

5. According to Matthew 26:39, Jesus was in submission to _____.
   a. His own will
   b. His Father's will
   c. the laws of Rome
   d. there laws of Israel

6. One of the trends of the natural, human life is _____.
   a. doing good
   b. loving justice
   c. doing evil
   d. being kind

7. Satan tries to make people think that they do not need _____.
   a. Christ's death
   b. are known by God
   c. are too great
   d. religion

8. Satan tempted Christ to try to keep Him _____.
   a. true to God's purpose
   b. away from Jerusalem
   c. hungry and thirsty
   d. from going to the Cross

9.. Jesus' first miracle was done in the city of _____.
   a. Nazareth
   b. Cana
   c. Jerusalem
   d. Capernaum

10. When Jesus raised the widow's son, John recognized that He was _____.
   a. a man of God
   b. a healer
   c. compassion
   d. a, b, and c

60

Acknowledging God as our Father encourages us _____.
a. not to pray
b. to expect what we want
c. not to worry
d. not to expect anything

1a. ☐
b. ☐
c. ☐
d. ☐

The Lords Prayer teaches us about _____.
a. ourselves
b. prayer
c. Jesus
d. trust

2a. ☐
b. ☐
c. ☐
d. ☐

The Lord's Prayer consists of an invocation, a conclusion, and _____.
a. seven petitions
b. three requests
c. five discourses
d. nine prayers

3a. ☐
b. ☐
c. ☐
d. ☐

The last request in the Lord's Prayer is _____.
a. even so come, Lord Jesus
b. lead us not into temptation
c. hallowed be thy name
d. forgive us our debts

4a. ☐
b. ☐
c. ☐
d. ☐

The Old Testament includes_____.
a. a model prayer
b. only private prayers
c. private and public prayers
d. only public prayers

5a. ☐
b. ☐
c. ☐
d. ☐

In the Biblical record the posture used least while praying is _____.
a. lying down
b. kneeling
c. sitting
d. standing

6a. ☐
b. ☐
c. ☐
d. ☐

When we become aware of God's holiness, we also become aware of our _____.
a. sinfulness
b. holiness
c. faith
d. worship

7a. ☐
b. ☐
c. ☐
d. ☐

Because salvation has been extended to the Gentiles, they should be _____.
a. proud
b. continually thankful
c. Jewish in life style
d. self-centered

8a. ☐
b. ☐
c. ☐
d. ☐

According to Matthew 6:8, God knows what things we have need of _____.
a. when we ask
b. before we ask
c. after we ask
d. after He asks

9a. ☐
b. ☐
c. ☐
d. ☐

If we regard iniquity in our hearts when we pray, the Lord will_____.
a. answer us slowly
b. not be concerned
c. answer us quickly
d. not hear us

10a. ☐
b. ☐
c. ☐
d. ☐

1. Sin is a lack of conformity to _____.
   a. God's moral law
   b. natural law
   c. God's ceremonial law
   d. international law

2. The inward thought of hatred is the same as the outward act of _____.
   a. prejudice
   b. murder
   c. stealing
   d. adultery

3. We are sinners because _____.
   a. we sin
   b. Satan tempted Eve
   c. Adam sinned
   d. Christ died

4. Jesus said (John 8:34), ".....Whosoever committeth sin is the servant of _____."
   a. sin
   b. Satan
   c. self
   d. death

5. As our Priest, Christ provides intercession and _____.
   a. atonement
   b. the kingdom
   c. revelation
   d. prophecies

6. *Conversion* means _____.
   a. *regeneration*
   b. *to be born again*
   c. *a change of mind*
   d. *a change in direction*

7. Salvation comes only through _____.
   a. faith in Christ
   b. repentance
   c. conviction
   d. keeping the Law

8. Repentance is a change of _____.
   a. direction
   b. activity
   c. mind
   d. clothing

9. Bible reading, praying, worshiping, and witnessing are ways of _____.
   a. attaining salvation
   b. knowing God
   c. growing in grace
   d. making friends

10. Christians must keep themselves _____.
    a. from Satan
    b. from sin
    c. saved
    d. from temptation

802

1a. [
b. [
c. [
d. [

2a. [
b. [
c. [
d. [

3a. [
b. [
c. [
d. [

4a. [
b. [
c. [
d. [

5a.
b.
c.
d.

6a.
b.
c.
d.

7a.
b.
c.
d.

8a.
b.
c.
d.

9a.
b.
c.
d.

10a.
b.
c.
d.

God demonstrates His justice by _____.
a. hearing our prayers
b. being merciful to us
c. saving sinners
d. judging righteously

1a. ☐
b. ☐
c. ☐
d. ☐

The first instance of God's justice applied to man concerned _____.
a. Adam and Eve
b. Abraham
c. Sodom and Gomorrah
d. Egypt

2a. ☐
b. ☐
c. ☐
d. ☐

God's immutability causes Christians to be _____.
a. encouraged in prayer
b. healed in sickness
c. broken in spirit
d. overlooked

3a. ☐
b. ☐
c. ☐
d. ☐

The immutability of God gives Christians a sense of _____.
a. dread
b. fear
c. assurance
d. nourished in body

4a. ☐
b. ☐
c. ☐
d. ☐

God's existence is outside of our _____.
a. universe
b. concept of time
c. bodies
d. comprehension

5a. ☐
b. ☐
c. ☐
d. ☐

The Word of God (the Son) existed with God _____.
a. before Creation
b. after Creation
c. after the Resurrection
d. before the Transformation

6a. ☐
b. ☐
c. ☐
d. ☐

God demonstrates His love to all men today by sending _____.
a. His Son
b. His angels
c. the Spirit
d. the rain

7a. ☐
b. ☐
c. ☐
d. ☐

The greatest love ever shown was_____.
a. Adam's love for Eve
b. Christ dying for sinners
c. first-century Christian love
d. Jesus' love for John

8a. ☐
b. ☐
c. ☐
d. ☐

Our love for God is revealed by our _____.
a. love for Jesus
b. testimony
c. love for our brother
d. good works

9a. ☐
b. ☐
c. ☐
d. ☐

The type of love that Christians should show toward one another is presented in _____.
a. John Chapter 15
b. Matthew, Chapter 1
c. First Corinthians, Chapter 13
d. Third John, Chapter 2

10a. ☐
b. ☐
c. ☐
d. ☐

804

1a. [
b. [
c. [
d. [

2a. [
b. [
c. [
d. [

3a.
b.
c.
d.

4a.
b.
c.
d.

5a.
b.
c.
d.

6a.
b.
c.
d.

7a.
b.
c.
d.

8a.
b.
c.
d.

9a.
b.
c.
d.

10a.
b.
c.
d.

1. The bishop of Rome (92 to 101) who wrote *Epistle to the Corinthians* was _____.
   a. Ignatius
   b. Clement
   c. Peter
   d. Paul

2. The church fathers saw no distinction between the authority of _____.
   a. the Bible and the church
   b. the Old and New Testaments
   c. the Spirit and the pastors
   d. Peter and Nero

3. Apologists were men who wrote to _____.
   a. defend the Faith
   b. condemn Rome
   c. Apollos
   d. all the churches

4. The father of systematic theology was _____.
   a. Paul
   b. Tertullian
   c. Athanasius
   d. Ireneaus

5. The first person who can accurately be given the title *pope* was _____.
   a. Urban II
   b. Boniface
   c. Gregory
   d. Charlemagne

6. Efforts by the Roman Church to free the Holy Land from Muslim control were called _____.
   a. wars
   b. missionary journeys
   c. liberation movements
   d. crusades

7. Zwingli, a Catholic priest, said that the sole authority for Christians was the _____.
   a. Bible
   b. pope
   c. Roman church
   d. Holy Spirit

8. The author of *The Institutes of Christian religion* was _____.
   a. Zwingli
   b. Huss
   c. Luther
   d. Calvin

9. The Reformation in England began in the year _____.
   a. 1517
   b. 1096
   c. 1610
   d. 1534

10. The person responsible for translating the Bible for English speakers was _____.
    a. Luther
    b. Tyndale
    c. Tudor
    d. Calvin

Jesus was born during the reign of the first Roman emperor, _____.
a. Tiberius
b. Nero
c. Pilate
d. Augustus

The civilizing force of Rome was the _____.
a. army
b. consul
c. senate
d. equites

After the death of David's son, Solomon, the kingdom of Israel _____.
a. ceased to exist
b. was never independent
c. was divided
d. grew

After the Babylonian Exile, the center of Jewish worship was the _____.
a. Tabernacle
b. synagogue
c. home
d. church

The disciple chosen to replace Judas as one of the Twelve was _____.
a. Matthias
b. Joseph
c. Barsabas
d. Justus

After the disciples were filled with the Holy Spirit on the day of Pentecost, they spoke of the _____.
a. Gospel message
b. need for repentance
c. death of Christ
d. wonderful works of God

The Christians in the Jerusalem church _____.
a. stayed in Jerusalem
b. lived in harmony
c. shared all things
d. were led by Paul

The first Jerusalem deacon to be martyred was _____.
a. Philip
b. Stephen
c. Nicanor
d. Timon

Philip was instrumental in the conversion of many _____.
a. eunuchs
b. Gentiles
c. Samaritans
d. Jews

The Apostle who first went to the Gentiles with the message of Christ was _____.
a. Paul
b. Philip
c. Peter
d. Barnabas

1. The first stop on Paul's first missionary journey was _____.
   a. Cyprus
   b. Crete
   c. Ephesus
   d. Perga

2. Paul was stoned and left for dead at _____.
   a. Perga
   b. Antioch of Pisidia
   c. Derbe
   d. Lystra

3. The principal city of Macedonia where Paul and Silas were imprisoned was _____.
   a. Thessalonica
   b. Athens
   c. Corinth
   d. Philippi

4. On his second missionary journey Paul stayed a year and a half in _____.
   a. jail
   b. Athens
   c. Corinth
   d. Ephesus

5. In Rome, Paul stayed almost two years in _____.
   a. jail
   b. the ship
   c. Melita
   d. Crete

6. Paul lived in Rome in a _____.
   a. jail
   b. palace
   c. rented house
   d. synagogue

7. The person whom Paul left in Ephesus to help to establish that church was _____.
   a. Titus
   b. Timothy
   c. Silas
   d. Barnabas

8. The Ephesians church was greatly disrupted by _____.
   a. Demas and Alexander
   b. Demas and Candia
   c. Hymenaeus and Demas
   d. Hymenaeus and Alexander

9. Provincial governors were ordered to persecute Christians by the Roman emperor _____.
   a. Nero
   b. Trojan
   c. Julius Caesar
   d. Augustus

10. The early Christian churches met to worship in _____.
    a. synagogues
    b. the city streets
    c. homes
    d. the Temple

Numerical proverbs state a number in the first line and increase it in the second line by _____.
a. one
b. two
c. three
d. nothing

1a. ☐
b. ☐
c. ☐
d. ☐

The word *mashal* (proverb) literally means _____.
a. *to rule*
b. *an example*
c. *to be like*
d. *a lesson*

2a. ☐
b. ☐
c. ☐
d. ☐

The first section of the three sections of Proverbs can be entitled Solomon's _____.
a. first collection of proverbs
b. second collection of proverbs
c. proverbial poems
d. collection of poems

3a. ☐
b. ☐
c. ☐
d. ☐

Solomon had all of these objectives in his proverbs *except* _____.
a. to know wisdom
b. to know poetry
c. to give to the simple
d. to know instruction

4a. ☐
b. ☐
c. ☐
d. ☐

The New Testament quotes Proverbs _____.
a. seventeen times
b. only once
c. seven times
d. four times

5a. ☐
b. ☐
c. ☐
d. ☐

Compared with lessons in Proverbs, some New Testament teachings are _____.
a. contradictory
b. parallel
c. more acceptable
d. more inspired

6a. ☐
b. ☐
c. ☐
d. ☐

The book of James is sometimes called the New Testament _____.
a. Proverbs
b. book of life
c. wisdom book
d. summarized

7a. ☐
b. ☐
c. ☐
d. ☐

Proverbs and James both deal with _____.
a. temper
b. prophecy
c. worship
d. inheritance

8a. ☐
b. ☐
c. ☐
d. ☐

The key phrase in Proverbs is _____.
a. the beginning of wisdom
b. depart from foolishness
c. to know wisdom
d. fear of the Lord

9a. ☐
b. ☐
c. ☐
d. ☐

The proverbs restated word for word include all of the topics *except* _____.
a. youth
b. religion
c. gossip
d. marriage

10a. ☐
b. ☐
c. ☐
d. ☐

☐

1. The Bible gives answers to life's dilemmas through all of these *except* _____.
   a. positive commands
   b. neutral commands
   c. negative commands
   d. guiding principles

2. Christians should follow behavior that causes another Christian to be _____.
   a. edified
   b. persuaded
   c. judged
   d. imitated

3. A drug is a substance that affects the body's _____.
   a. physical coordination
   b. nervous system
   c. sinful acts
   d. Creation

4. Many young people take illegal drugs to _____.
   a. help them to sleep
   b. be better Christians
   c. defy gravity
   d. defy authority

5. Enduring friendships can only develop between people who share the same _____.
   a. last name
   b. leisure-time activities
   c. life values and perspective
   d. personality traits

6. "A friend loveth _____."
   a. in adversity
   b. at all times
   c. greatly
   d. enough to borrow

7. To study effectively, a student should follow all these steps *except* _____.
   a. select carefully where to sit
   b. plan deadlines for every project
   c. concentrate well in class
   d. cram thoroughly for a test

8. When a student is tempted to cheat, God will always _____.
   a. stop the temptation
   b. not allow him to cheat
   c. not interfere
   d. make a way to escape cheating

9. In all decisions, Christians should commit themselves to all of these items *except* the _____.
   a. rule of peace
   b. rule of feeling
   c. word of Christ
   d. plan of God

10. To avoid procrastination you should do all of these activities *except* _____.
    a. establish step priority
    b. dwell on the matter
    c. set clear goals
    d. plan each step

1a. [
b. [
c. [
d. [

2a. [
b. [
c. [
d. [

3a. [
b. [
c. [
d. [

4a.
b.
c.
d.

5a.
b.
c.
d.

6a.
b.
c.
d.

7a.
b.
c.
d.

8a.
b.
c.
d.

9a.
b.
c.
d.

10a.
b.
c.
d.

Human parents are extremely careful to ensure their child's _____.
a. survival
b. future
c. education
d. health

1a. ☐
b. ☐
c. ☐
d. ☐

Parents will gradually release some of their protective supervision as the child approaches _____.
a. his first birthday
b. second grade
c. marriage
d. adolescence

2a. ☐
b. ☐
c. ☐
d. ☐

Although Abraham loved Isaac, he _____.
a. sacrificed him
b. did not love Ishmael
c. had no children
d. loved God more

3a. ☐
b. ☐
c. ☐
d. ☐

When Jesus called God "Father", He was emphasizing God's _____.
a. discipline
b. character
c. nearness
d. sterness

4a. ☐
b. ☐
c. ☐
d. ☐

Children are consumers of these items *except* _____.
a. goods
b. instruction
c. life
d. responsibility

5a. ☐
b. ☐
c. ☐
d. ☐

The Bible commands children to be _____.
a. happy
b. quiet
c. obedient
d. mature

6a. ☐
b. ☐
c. ☐
d. ☐

A substitute parent that requires no interaction is _____.
a. television
b. a grandparent
c. a baby sitter
d. a friend

7a. ☐
b. ☐
c. ☐
d. ☐

Two young people who substituted peers for parents were _____.
a. Joseph and Benjamin
b. Joshua and Caleb
c. Hohpni and Phinehas
d. Jeroboam and Rehoboam

8a. ☐
b. ☐
c. ☐
d. ☐

One of the most common of organized activities for a family to share is _____.
a. eating a meal
b. camping out
c. a vacation trip
d. going to church

9a. ☐
b. ☐
c. ☐
d. ☐

Tastes in sports, music, art, and literature are taught _____.
a. casually
b. only by parents
c. informally
d. formally

10a. ☐
b. ☐
c. ☐
d. ☐

1. The Lord's Prayer was given as a _____.
   a. sermon
   b. model
   c. ritual
   d. prayer

2. Jesus is the prophesied Priest, King, and _____.
   a. Prince
   b. Person
   c. Mediator
   d. Prophet

3. Because God is immutable, He never _____.
   a. speaks loudly
   b. dies
   c. changes
   d. remembers sin

4. Travel in the Roman Empire was made safe and easy by the _____.
   a. four-horse chariot
   b. Roman senate
   c. Pax Romana
   d. Roman aqueducts

5. The city from which Barnabas and Paul launched their missionary activity was _____.
   a. Antioch
   b. Jerusalem
   c. Caesarea
   d. Tarsus

6. The Jerusalem Conference concerned whether Gentiles _____.
   a. could be saved
   b. should be circumcised
   c. could marry Jews
   d. should eat pork

7. On his third missionary journey Paul stayed almost three years in _____.
   a. jail
   b. Greece
   c. Macedonia
   d. Ephesus

8. Being personally persuaded, not judging others, not being a stumbling block, surrendering personal right, and glorifying God are _____.
   a. positive commands
   b. neutral commands
   c. negative commands
   d. guiding principles

9. The old nature is derived from _____.
   a. the flesh
   b. Adam
   c. sinful acts
   d. Creation

10. Students who cheat do so because they usually are _____.
    a. trying to please the Lord
    b. excellent students
    c. too lazy to study
    d. unaware that cheating is wrong